Let's Take Stock

LET'S TAKE STOCK

An Inside Look at Wall Street

By
DON G. CAMPBELL

the NEW Bobbs-Merrill COMPANY, INC.
AN ASSOCIATE OF HOWARD W. SAMS & CO., INC.
Publishers • INDIANAPOLIS • NEW YORK

COPYRIGHT © 1959 BY THE BOBBS-MERRILL COMPANY, INC.
PRINTED IN THE UNITED STATES OF AMERICA

FIRST EDITION

LIBRARY OF CONGRESS CATALOG CARD NUMBER: 59-14299

Introduction

THERE are many times—now, for one—when the idea that anyone in his right mind would sit down and read a book about the stock market is enough to curl the hair on the back of a man's head. What's happened to the good, old, wholesome hobbies that used to keep people down in the basement at all hours working with their hands? What's happened, for example, to all the people who used to make those corner knick-knack shelves?

Life, it seems, has grown awfully Earnest and, somehow or other, the fetish of making Big Money without lifting a pinkie in the process has become all the rage. Twenty years of listening to the dreary old saw about the grasshopper and the ant has suddenly exploded in our faces in a sort of pro-grasshopper, anti-ant philosophy. This attitude, while it may be a lot of fun, is supposed to be pretty naughty, and there has sprung up a dedicated little band of writers (or "hacks") who have set themselves the noble task of informing the public that the stock market is not for grasshoppers but only for ants of sober substance. All of which may come as a big shock to thousands of grasshoppers on Wall Street who have had a very fat thing for years in this making of money without doing anything for it.

This book is based on the theory that the reader wants to learn what stocks are, what the stock market is and what it is all supposed to mean to him personally. (Frankly, this last point never gets answered, but no book is perfect, you know.)

It will not tell you how to get rich, but it will explain how some people have done it. It will also give you several invaluable pointers on how you can lose everything short of your contact lenses in less time than it takes to say: "You're faded!"

But, perhaps of more interest, it tries to tell you how you can invest in stocks with a minimum of risk (if that's what you want), a little bit of risk (if that's what you want), or a lot of risk (if *that's* what you want). It gets into the Monthly Investment Plan, the how's of setting up an investment club, mutual funds and all sorts of jolly things like that. It is, at times, impossibly dull.

For help in putting this thing together with, let's trust, a minimum of flubs, we must offer our deepest thanks to two extremely patient gentlemen: Alex S. Carroll of the Indianapolis office of Thomson and McKinnon brokerage, and E. George Schaefer, publisher of *The Dow Theory Trader*. Both were much too polite, really, to say what they thought.

Contents

CHAPTER		PAGE
1.	Astride a Fat Pig—To Market, to Market	11
2.	"So, What's in It for Me?"	19
3.	"The Kindly Broker"	27
4.	The "Perfect" Stock and Other Fables	33
5.	Heavy Stuff: The "Senior" Equities	41
6.	One Foot in the Boat: Income and Growth	47
7.	Luck, Pluck and Crossed Fingers: The Growth Stocks	53
8.	Russo-American Roulette: How to Speculate	59
9.	Rocks of Ages: The Blue Chips	69
10.	"Togetherness": Mutual Funds	75
11.	A Place on "The Big Board"	83
12.	Party! Party! The Investment Clubs	89
13.	The Solitary Dabbler: The MIP	97
14.	The Sinking Ship: When to Sell	103
15.	Hedging Your Bets	109
16.	The Haggle Market: Over-the-Counter Stocks	119
17.	How to Be a Sorehead: Selling Short	125
18.	Signs, Symbols and Tiny Type	131
19.	Palmistry and Head Bumps: The Seers	141
20.	Technical Studies: Reading the Pulse	149
	Brief Topical Index	159

Let's Take Stock

1

Astride a Fat Pig—
To Market, to Market

THIS BOOK is based on the assumption that you don't have a million dollars, but that you turn pea-green at the mention of anyone who does have a million dollars.

At the same time it also presumes that you can count up to ten without blacking out, that you give at least a passing thought to that great day when you can drop the job down at the baseball-stitching plant, and retire to breed piranha fish, and that you realize that saving and investing money doesn't necessarily make you a freak of some kind.

In short, the book has to do with making a buck.

To lay it on the line, no one these days except the Federal government and the Blue Fairy who lives at the bottom of our garden ever puts his money into a commercial project without entertaining the—at least vague—hope of making something on the deal.

Down at the pool hall they like to call this "the profit motive," and, if it were as sinful as some people like to paint it, we Americans would still be trying to explain away the price we paid for Manhattan. Fortunately, the hope of making money by investing it in another man's talents, or business skill, needs no apology in this country in spite of the wild-eyed efforts in some quarters to make the whole thing seem about as *tsk*-provoking as clubbing old ladies.

The theory, though, does need some light shed on it, particularly as it applies to the stock market, which is not only the most basically "American" form of investment available to us, but also the least understood and—it follows—one of the most mistrusted.

Today, a very fat 12,490,000 people in this country own common stocks and there probably aren't more than 10 of them who still wear plug hats, smoke two-dollar cigars and beat their liveried footmen. In contrast, of every 100 stockholders in the country today, a fat 55 of them earn $7,500, or less, a year—about nine of them having incomes of less than $58 a week, about 20 having incomes of $59 to $96 a week and another 26 of them having incomes of $97 to $145 a week. Not quite 45 of every 100 stockholders today can boast of incomes greater than $7,500 a year. It's a rich man's game in about the same way craps is.

As long as we're knocking holes in time-honored arguments, we might as well blow up, too, the idea that stock ownership is reserved for somber, steady gentlemen of mellow years. Better than one out of every five stockholders today, as a matter of fact, is in the relatively fuzz-cheeked, 21-to-34 year age group. Like running around with girls, it's something you can't start too soon.

In all, about one out of every eight adult Americans owns stock, the highest figure in history. Yet, it's a figure that could be tripled or quadrupled to everyone's advantage if it weren't for a general misunderstanding of what in the name of Betsy the whole subject of stocks is all about, and if it weren't for certain hangovers from a day in 1929 when the stock market got hit with a bag of bolts.

Astride a Fat Pig—To Market, to Market

The stock market, contrary to your sour Uncle Josh who dropped $200 in dirigible stock back in 1919 and hasn't forgotten it, is *not* a lot of things: it's not a game of showdown poker; it's not a way to make a fast buck; it's not a sucker trap in which Wall Street czars—whoever *they* might be—pull strings and cause the market to bobble up and down like a lie-detector needle strapped to Nikita Khrushchev's arm.

A share of stock, oddly, is just what it says it is—a share of a business' hopes, plans and accomplishments. If you buy a share of General Motors, you're not buying just an ornate piece of very good, crinkly paper, but a very real 1/280,840,000th of what General Motors has left over each year after it has subtracted from its tremendous gross income a certain percentage for taxes, reserves, labor, materials, advertising, research and expansion. The whole thing is about as mysterious as making a theater reservation.

Naturally, anybody who says you can't lose money on the stock market has sinister motives and, in a recent survey, about 60 per cent of the people noted this fact as their major reason for distrusting common stocks as an investment. Forgotten, apparently, is the fact that you can lose money just as fast on a chicken farm, your home, the depreciation on your car, loans to your in-laws, or simply standing there, counting your pocket change over a sidewalk grating.

You can lay odds on it: if there's absolutely no risk in the investment, then you've got something by the tail that's pretty dead—and pretty unprofitable, too. You might as well write a policy on a church bazaar insuring them against maritime accidents.

Being willing to take a slight chance with his money, though, doesn't make an individual a potential investor any more than having two legs makes him a hopscotch champion. The flat truth is that a lot of people who would like to invest in stocks shouldn't at this time, and still others should never invest in them.

It makes sense, of course, that stocks should not be substituted for savings, life insurance, home ownership or some degree of investment in other, more liquid, assets such as government bonds. Some authorities even go so far as to say that you shouldn't buy a penny's worth of stock until you're in the position where you can lay your hands on enough cash to make up half of your annual income. Hah! Realistically, today's taxes and cost of living—plus the fact that stock ownership should be started as soon in life as possible—makes a goal like this desirable but highly unlikely.

One rule of thumb on how much cash, or easily converted assets, you should have on hand before shopping around in the stock market is based on this bit of soul-searching: run back over your personal affairs last year and figure how much you had to spend out of your savings for unexpected expenses—the broken leg you hadn't planned on, the 300-dollar lawn mower that blew up in the middle of the grass season, the dental braces that flipped apart in your daughter's mouth and propped it open like a trapped alligator's, and so on. Take this figure and triple it. Normally this will give you a good idea of how much safety reserve you'll need—barring the possibility that your garage will be hit by a meteor.

Quite apart from the risk that exists in stock ownership, such a cash reserve is needed so that—in case of emergency—you won't have to sell your stock, possibly at a sacrifice price, just to buy your son out of car-stripping charges.

And, it has to be sadly admitted, some people are no more emotionally suited to be stockholders than they are to walk high wires; they are the worriers who flutter at every jiggle of

Astride a Fat Pig—To Market, to Market

the market, drive both themselves and their brokers crazy, and turn to compulsive eating to get their minds on something else.

Their big worry, of course, is that "The Market" will suddenly pounce on them, snatch their life savings away and then ride off into the darkness like a Lone Ranger turned crooked. This fascination of looking at "The Market" as some sort of big blob cracking a whip isn't confined to the worriers, but can be found even among the constantly grinning optimists who similarly view "It"—The Market—as a sort of cross between Santa Claus and Daddy Warbucks.

Actually "The Market," as such, doesn't buy anything, doesn't sell anything and has no more to do with the actual selling prices of stocks than Zip the Pin-Headed Boy. It's a market place, pure and simple, and except for the plumbing the New York Stock Exchange today is startlingly similar in operation to what it was back in the 1700s when the handful of financiers then living in New York stood around under an old buttonwood tree and haggled over the few securities then in existence.

In 1792, twenty-four of these snuff-pinching brokers drew up an agreement that was to provide the foundation for the present New York Stock Exchange, moved into a near-by coffeehouse to get out of the rain, and set up an informal shop there. From then on, the Stock Exchange changed its address almost as fast as its members changed socks and it wasn't until 1865 that it moved into permanent quarters at 10-12 Broad Street.

In all honesty one has to admit that things got pretty wild in the early days as the country began bursting at the seams and as hundreds of new stock issues hit the market. Respectability—as in the case of a dance-hall madam who has found "Mr. Right"—came along at a considerably slower pace but, gradually, new and sometimes radical rules laid down by the Exchange began blunting the knife-in-the-back tactics. The old swindle of issuing a public bloc of stock and then watering it to death with a secret issue was killed off, and finally the officers of the Exchange managed to knock off the vicious "bucket-shops" that had clung to it like a pack of jackals.

These sucker traps, which posed as "brokerages," preyed on the little man and were roughly on an ethical par with a floating crap game. For half a buck you bought a chance on a listed stock and either won yourself a dollar or lost your "investment" on the basis of the stock's fluctuations that particular day. The numbers racket adopted the idea later and put it on a curb-service basis.

Today, the Exchange's rules are tighter than a wet two-dollar hat, and any stock that makes the "Big Board"—has been approved for listing on the Exchange—has been gone over like the application of an 85-year-old for life insurance. A listing on the Exchange doesn't mean that a company can't fall flat on its face or suffer from bad management. It does mean that it's no fly-by-night outfit dreamed up by an out-of-work black-jack dealer; it is a respectable company with a background of successful operation, which is duty-bound to make public everything but its Wasserman.

And when you buy that company's stock you're doing, in effect, what the boys in 1792 did out under the buttonwood tree—only without the "prithees" and "by your leaves." Here's what happens:

We'll say that under a stone in your fireplace you've found a mysterious tin box that contains $11,000 in cash, a revolver with two empty chambers and a floor plan of the neighborhood bank—a windfall of sorts, you might say. Let's also say that you've heard something favorable about Freeport Sulphur and decide to invest your $11,000 in that company after talking

Astride a Fat Pig—To Market, to Market

over the problem with your broker. Acting for you, the broker teletypes to New York and learns that Freeport is currently selling at 107⅞ bid, 109⅛ asked. This simply means that the brokers on the floor at the Exchange who are trying to sell shares of Freeport for their customers are trying to make a price of $109.125 a share on it, while those brokers commissioned to buy it for their customers (or for themselves) are trying to chisel the price down to $107.875 a share. They aren't there to make friends of each other, you know. Obviously, they'll end up either compromising on this apparent impasse or locked in a fist fight.

Having the situation well in mind, your broker suggests to you that you try to pick it up at $108.875 (108⅞) a share but, failing there, to buy it for $109. Once the order to this effect is relayed to New York, your broker's representative on the Exchange floor goes to the trading post where Freeport is traded (one of 18 such posts) and sounds out the other brokers assembled on the sentiment surrounding Freeport. After learning the range of bids, he offers to anyone around the trading post who is in a position to hear him a bid of 108⅞ for Freeport. There is, to put it politely, a stony silence. A few minutes later he bids again—this time at a flat 109. This flushes out a seller who knows a good thing when he hears it and who decisively shouts back: "Sold! One hundred at one-oh-nine!"

The two brokers huddle, note their transactions and report them back to their clients; the transaction goes on the familiar ticker network as "FT 109" (meaning 100 shares sold at 109 of Freeport Sulphur—FT being Freeport's symbol).

Clerks in the respective offices finish the transaction and the seller of the stock turns in his certificates to the broker who, in turn, relays it to the bank which acts as Freeport's transfer agent. A new certificate for 100 shares of Freeport is issued to you and should hit your mailbox in about 10 days after the fuss on the Exchange floor.

Basically, at least, it's about as mysterious as the footnotes in a first-grade primer. You'll find the same sort of transaction going on at farm auctions all over the country as one man dickers for another's surplus cream separator—a haggle over price and then a compromise.

There's probably only one thing troubling you: Why bother?

2

"So, What's in It for Me?"

Fun is fun, and all that, but when you get right down to the wire, no one with some money firmly grasped in his hot little hand and with an eye on the future is prepared to laugh off the possibility of losing his poke. And, in this day and age, the ways of making money are probably outnumbered ten to one by the ways of losing it. Just standing there with a handful of greenbacks, for instance, is almost as good a way to lose it as feeding it to the pigeons.

Oh, ho! But money's money, isn't it, and—given the right humidity conditions—shouldn't a bank note hold up for at least 20 or 30 years in relatively good shape? It should, and there was a time in this country when it most certainly did hold up. But, as painful as it is to admit, times have changed, inflation has become a way of national life and—indignant protests from Washington to the contrary—there is little on the horizon to indicate that anything short of a major economic crisis is likely to change it.

In dear old Granddad's day, of course, being frugal was not only not considered anti-state—as it seems to be today—but it was even possible. In the case of your grandfather, for instance, the good gentleman found it possible to tuck away modest sums from time to time, and, at retirement, the income from stocks, bonds and rental real estate gave him an annual stipend of—to pluck an example—a princely $5,000.

To duplicate the scale today on which Grandfather lived in retirement back in the late 1930s—after all, look what's happened to the price of dandelion wine alone—we would need almost $12,000 a year, not $5,000. How, pray, does one retire today on an annual income of $12,000 a year? Very simple! You merely invest something like $230,000 in good, sound stocks. This is quite a pile by anyone's standards. If you hope to accumulate it in the 25 years remaining to you before retirement I'm sorry to report that your annual savings will have to average about $4,900—which, by the usual standards of savings, means that you're going to have to drop what you're doing now and get out and find yourself a $24,000-a-year job. Find two, while you're at it.

It's an ugly fact of life that the $1,000 that you slipped into the sugar bowl back in 1940 is now worth about $504 in actual purchasing power. On top of that, the sugar's turned lumpy, too.

At this point the temptation is one of throwing up the hands, dashing out and buying a 15-dollar bottle of Scotch and forgetting the whole mess. Despite the Federal government's noble efforts to reduce us all to a placid state of mediocre dependency on the state in future years, we can, with some astute planning, raise our retirement standard of living to, if not the rosy $12,000-a-year level, at least a moderate improvement over the stark existence promised by our Social Security checks. The answer lies in systematic savings, and in careful investment of the small funds that the skyrocketing living costs and taxes have not been able to wring out of us.

The art of saving is an intensely personal thing, of course, that—like banjo plucking—isn't picked up overnight. And, the art of knowing how to put those savings to work, once you've

"So, What's in It for Me?"

accumulated them, is an even harder chore. They go hand in hand, though, and there's no point in getting all satiated with shrewd investment theories if you're not prepared to make the personal sacrifices that are necessary to implement them—barring the possibility here, of course, that you may have a very rich uncle with a lingering chest cold.

Assuming that you are prepared to cut down on exotic hair dressings and brush your own teeth without a dental technician standing by, the experts in this field say that you should be able to tuck away between 8 and 15 per cent of your annual income if you are single and earning about $4,000 a year. A family of four, living on a $6,000-a-year income, naturally won't do as well and shouldn't even try to put away more than 5 per cent of its income a year. All of this is extremely elastic, of course, and will largely depend on the degree of importance that your family assigns to: (1) future comfort, (2) immediate comfort, and (3) a natural gamble on eventualities, sometimes known as the "what-the-hell!" philosophy.

However you rank these factors, it's probably safe to assume that the problem of providing yourself with a comfortable retirement income in an age of inflation, high taxes and other economic uncertainties is beginning to nag you. A worry that isn't exactly quieted any by the knowledge that:

1. Only one out of every 13 people now age 65 or more is financially independent.

2. Only seven out of every 100 people over age 65 have incomes of $5,000 a year or more.

3. Nearly 75 per cent of those people over age 65 have either no income at all, or receive less than $1,000 a year—less than $19.23 a week, that is.

Simply sticking a given amount of money into your mattress every year, unfortunately, isn't going to make you any better off than the majority of today's retired people because, frankly, at the present rate of depreciation of the dollar, your mattress—in another 20 years—could end up being of more value as a collector's item than the money you stuck in it. The money you are beginning to save today must appreciate in value over the next 20 or 25 years—it's that simple.

Banks, savings and loan institutions and insurance do, of course, pay dividends and offer a large share of safety—thanks to governmental regulations and insured deposits. For this safety, though, we pay rather heavily by having to accept lower interest rates—from $1\frac{1}{2}$ to 3 per cent—and in quite a few recent years the increasing sickness of the dollar has been sufficient to more than wipe out such interest rates.

This certainly doesn't mean that a good chunk of your savings shouldn't go into such investments. Money on deposit in banks and in savings and loan companies has a charming attribute—you can get your big hands on it in a couple of hours if necessary. And, by all means, keep fully insured even though this sort of investment—being tied to a fixed return on the money—may, indeed, drag along behind the increase in the cost of living. Happily, it gives your family instant protection from the moment your application is approved, which is something that no stock-investment plan can approach.

But, for the type of investment program that has the best chance of keeping up with or ahead of inflation, we don't have much choice but to return to the subject of common stocks. Why this is so is usually dismissed with the airy explanation that stocks "go up."

Aside from skipping rather gaily over the fact that stocks also "go down," the explanation is a bit more dramatic than it is sensible. To understand why stocks usually keep pace with inflation we must drag out a homey little example of how it all

"So, What's in It for Me?"

comes about. The crux of it is that your return on a common stock is based on a share in a business in fixed dollars.

We'll say that, today, you've got a little stock in a firm that sells air-conditioned bait buckets. From this sort of foolishness the company earns about $1,000,000 a year, or about $1 a share (based largely on the fact that the buckets sell for $15 apiece).

Inflation hits, of course, and it becomes necessary year by year to raise the price of the buckets until they sell for $45 apiece. An outrageous price until you realize that haircuts, too, have gone up to $4.50 and that a cup of coffee in a restaurant sells for 40 cents—and don't laugh, the day may yet come. If your return on this investment were geared to a flat $1 a share you would, obviously, be in pretty bad shape. Fortunately, the company—now with earnings of about $3,000,000 a year—sticks to its policy of tying dividends to earnings and you find yourself collecting $3 a share.

Maybe, when all is said and done, you've no more than kept up with the cost of living, but you've at least accomplished what is rapidly becoming a near impossibility.

At this point—from the back of the room—there comes from the giggling stag line a few catcalls and hooting criticisms: (1) stocks can go down as well as up, and (2) simply because we've had a few years of inflation there is no reason for thinking it's an endless problem.

Stocks can, indeed, go down and stay down for long periods of time, but we are talking here about long-term investment—20 or 25 years—and in both this department, and in the newness of inflation, there is a lot of historical evidence to tout common stocks as an effective hedge against "dollar-rot."

One recent study of the problem took the 85 years between 1871 and 1956 and—for purposes of examination—broke it down into 56 overlapping 30-year periods (1871-1901; 1876-1906; 1881-1911, and so forth).

Of the 56 periods studied it was found that prices rose steadily throughout 52 of them, declined during two periods and remained unchanged during two periods. Whether they invested for one year or longer, then, investors have had inflation to cope with more than half the time since 1871, and over long 30-year periods since 1871 they've had inflation virtually all the time. In every one of these 30-year periods, happily, common-stock prices increased too.

For shorter investment periods the record isn't quite so good. The same 1871-1956 period was also studied one year at a time and in overlapping periods of 10, 15 and 20 (as well as the already mentioned 30) years. As a hedge against inflation it was found that common stocks worked best the longer they were held. Thus, the 30-year investor has seen his stocks climb in price during every one of the inflationary periods of the past 85 years. Ironically, the 10-year investor has fared almost as well and has seen stock prices climb in 98 per cent of the inflationary periods encountered.

Admittedly, the fact that prices of common stocks rise as living costs rise (in most cases) doesn't mean that they automatically keep up with living costs.

From a dividend standpoint, however, the returns on common stocks have at least kept up with living costs in from 75 to 88 per cent of the inflationary periods studied, and in many cases dividends have far outstripped the cost of living. Among the 30-year inflationary periods studied, for instance, dividends rose at least four times faster than the cost of living in 40 per cent of the cases, and at least two times faster in 88 per cent of the cases.

When prices of common stocks (and their dividends) haven't

kept pace with the cost of living, in practically every case these periods have come either at the tail end of terrifically inflationary periods or directly afterward in times of abnormally depressed stock prices.

There probably isn't any completely foolproof way of dodging inflation short of moving to an uncharted tropical isle and becoming self-sufficient with a herd of goats, a cow and a spinning wheel. Even then, it will cost you twice as much to get there as it did 10 years ago.

For the moment, common stocks shape up as the best bet.

3

"The Kindly Broker"

THE AVERAGE, or garden-variety, broker is inclined to be a somewhat dyspeptic gentleman with either a nervous squint from attempting to read one-inch-high stock quotations from the far side of a room or with a perennially bruised nose caused by slapping a pair of small field glasses to his eyes hour after hour. He normally lives in the suburbs, drives a late-model car and has a daughter who plays the piano.

A good part of the broker's chronic stomach trouble, of course, is a result of the strain that anyone suffers who is presumed to be infallible in his decisions and who is expected to possess an encyclopedic knowledge of every manufacturing firm in the United States, ranging in size from General Motors down to obscure little two-men partnerships that specialize in the fabrication of plastic shoestring tips.

For instance, put yourself in the place of a man who has just discouraged a small investor from sinking his life savings into Consolidated Lint on the grounds that the stock is unrealistically high priced. Having done this noble service, you and your client watch with awe as Consolidated Lint blithely leapfrogs upward in price while the stock you substituted for it quietly nose-dives to a new 20-year low.

Things like this—clients being the way they are—are enough to wear even a very strong man's nerves down eventually, especially if the client is the type who hangs around the brokerage all day muttering darkly to himself and casting withering looks in the broker's direction. Multiply by a dozen or two instances of cockeyed advice (everybody has days when nothing seems to go right!) and it's a wonder that brokers have any hair at all. In nervous wear and tear the average broker probably works harder during his relatively short business day than a demolition expert. Unfortunately there is no middle ground in his relationship with his clients—he's either a hero or a heel, depending on where the market seems to be heading on any particular day.

The word "broker" itself—which cynics frequently find very apt as a description of the condition in which the dealer in securities leaves them—goes back to the Norman days of early England when French was often spoken. Life then was a willy-nilly affair in which a man raised what he needed to eat and traded the surplus to neighbors for produce that wouldn't grow on his own land. This sort of fundamental economic existence left the village innkeeper as about the only man in the average Norman community with any practical experience in the actual buying and selling of property. It was natural, then, for a simple Norman farmer who didn't dig this business of selling, or buying, something for cash—instead of trading a cow, or his daughter's virtue, for it—to seek help from the village innkeeper. Since the innkeeper was the man who used a *broche*, or spigot, to tap his own wares, he was known as the local *brocheur*. And so, Anglicized, the "broker" became the man who bought and sold for his clients. Isn't that fascinating? Useless perhaps, but fascinating.

The complexities of the twentieth century being what they are, the basic job of the broker—to act as an agent for people

"The Kindly Broker"

wishing to buy securities—has been expanded until he now serves as a sort of Dutch uncle, father confessor, friendly advisor, researcher and alter ego for his clients. He is also expected to make a reasonable number of speeches before investment groups, act as a sort of "school sponsor" for investment clubs and generally keep himself available as a soft, sympathetic shoulder on which the worriers can occasionally weep. The whole thing requires no more tact and diplomacy than that needed by the head disciplinarian who has been assigned to make a gentleman out of an Arab sultan's untouchable, but spoiled, brat of a son.

For all of this the broker works either on a flat salary, or—more commonly—on a commission basis that is tied in with the commission his firm, in turn, charges the client. This commission doesn't make the broker quite the fat cat you might have imagined.

Actually the broker's commission for the buying and selling of securities is one of the lowest—in terms of percentages—charged by any industry for its services. It isn't an entirely fair comparison, perhaps, but the broker's commission is considerably less than the flat 5 per cent that you pay a real-estate broker for selling your home. Of course the house sale usually entails more running around, dickering and advertising than the securities broker encounters in selling 100 shares of Consolidated Pizza. However, since the securities broker's charge drops sharply with the size of the transaction there is a considerable dollar gap between what the security broker and the real-estate broker would each get for a transaction of the same size.

The commissions on securities are based strictly on the number of shares being bought or sold and on the prevailing market price of the stock. The broker himself isn't involved at all in the interesting, but immaterial, business of whether you are losing money, making money or breaking even on the transaction. Using the schedule of commissions which brokers have been operating under since mid-1958, then, here is what buying or selling a hundred shares of any stock will cost you (the dollar amount shown indicates the size of the total transaction, of course):

Under $100—commission here is on a mutual-agreement basis between the broker and the customer and normally works out at about 6 per cent.

Between $100 and $399———2 per cent plus $3.

Between $400 and $2,199———1 per cent plus $7.

Between $2,200 and $4,999———one-half of 1 per cent plus $19.

$5,000 and above———one-tenth of 1 per cent plus $39.

This, then, is what the brokerage commission would amount to on either a "buy" or "sell" order involving:

100 shares costing a total of $250———$5 plus $3, total: $8.

200 shares costing a total of $1,000———$10 plus $6, total: $16.

100 shares costing a total of $4,000———$20 plus $19, total: $39.

100 shares costing a total of $8,000———$40 plus $39, total: $79.

As mentioned before, all of these refer to transactions involving 100 shares of stock—a "round lot." A transaction involving fewer than 100 shares—and here, frankly, is where some of us have the most experience—is an "odd lot." Ironically, the actual commission rate charged by the broker for such a transaction is lower.

There's a difference in rates because of the fact that odd lot

"The Kindly Broker" 31

transactions have to be funneled by your broker through a specialist known as an "odd lot dealer." About the closest parallel you can draw here is to compare the odd lot dealer with a wholesaler. In this case the odd lot dealer buys stock in round lots and keeps them "on the shelf" to supply the demand for orders involving only 1, 5, 10, 13, 60 or 99 shares.

Not being in this strange business for his lung condition, the odd lot dealer makes his profit by selling odd lots at 12½ cents higher than the current market value (one-eight of a point, that is), and buying them at 12½ cents less than the market price. This arrangement applies to transactions involving stocks selling for less than $40 a share. Above $40 a share this differential is hiked to 25 cents a share in both directions (or one-quarter of a point).

Thus, if you buy 10 shares of a stock selling at 25⅜ ($25.375 a share) you are actually paying 25½ ($25.50 a share) because of the odd lot dealer's 12½-cent "drag."

Call it what you will, this is obviously a form of commission. To compensate for it, the commission that you would ordinarily pay your broker is shaved accordingly. The commission rate to him on odd lot transactions is thus the same as outlined above for round lot transactions except that $2 is subtracted from the total to compensate for the odd lot dealer's cut.

Applying this to the example given above in which you want to buy 10 shares of a stock costing 25⅜, then, the commission would be figured this way: since the odd lot dealer is charging you 25½ a share instead of the quoted 25⅜ he is, in effect, charging you $255 instead of the $253.73 you might expect. You're paying him a commission of $1.25. On top of this your own broker charges you on the basis of a $255 transaction and should normally collect $8.10. This, however, is reduced $2 because of the odd-lot dealer's compensation, so the whole bill for the transaction comes to $6.10, plus $1.25, or a total of $7.35. And . . .

Oh, but you're beginning to get nervous. Don't worry about it!

4

The "Perfect" Stock and Other Fables

ONCE upon a time there was a "perfect" stock—it yielded an annual dividend of about 10 per cent, it was as solid as a 290-pound left tackle, and it was increasing in value faster than a teenager outgrows his clothes.

It was, of course, a real estate holding firm known as Heaven, Inc., because that—regrettably—is the only place where such a situation could exist.

Life, unfortunately, is a real and earnest proposition, where the "perfect" stock has to be viewed in the same light as a 50-dollar mink stole: with considerable suspicion. There are "good" stocks, there are "excellent" stocks, and—within certain narrow specifications—there are some that in a careless moment might pass as "near-perfect." Needless to say, too, there are more "dogs" on the market than the Society for the Prevention of Cruelty to Animals has taken to its bosom in the history of that organization.

How a stock rates is a matter of personal definition. It boils down to a matter of what you alone want in a stock. After all, there are still a lot of people who consider Marilyn Monroe definitely on the hippy side, and the same odd differences in opinion run rampant on the stock market.

Do you, above all else, want a stable stock? Do you want a high-yielding stock? Do you want a stock that pays peanuts now but promises to grow over the years and increase considerably in value? Or do you like Amalgamated Ordinary Wash Day Products—not because you think that it could manufacture its way out of a wet tissue sack, but simply because you think that there are enough other idiots around who *do* think so who will push the price up for a quick killing?

It doesn't take tea leaves at this point to know what you're thinking, and the answer is a flat, uncompromising "No!" You can't have all four in the same stock, or—except in a few very, very rare cases—even two of these characteristics in the same stock. It's a hard choice to make—stability *vs.* income *vs.* growth *vs.* speculation—and while you're not going to put all your eggs in one basket, we trust, you will still be faced with the decision of building the major part of your investment program around one of these goals.

There are several considerations that you should go into making up your mind: your age, your earning capacity and its future potential, your current resources and the responsibilities that you are likely to assume in the future.

The decision is a hard one because—as in picking a bride—there's a liability offsetting every asset involved in the matter of stock selection. If you want stability above all else, you will have to sacrifice some of the income you might get from other stocks to get this security. If you're interested in a high yield—and who in this world isn't to a certain extent?—you can get a fair shake in this department, but you'll have to kiss off some stability in attaining it. If you want growth, you'll have to give up the idea of a high yield and cross your fingers in the hope that you've picked a real growth stock and not just a bunch of guys in white laboratory coats posing for pictures to be used in the company's annual report—who only *look* as if they're developing wonderful new products.

Really stable—which is almost synonymous with "mature"—firms pay a relatively modest dividend (around 3 to 4 per cent) but have a long record of guessing right about what will sell, during which their earnings may or may not have shown a slight steady improvement.

High-income companies, on the other hand, are practically always grouped in the cyclical industries—automobiles, heavy equipment, steel, farm machinery and so forth, the sort of things that sell in boom periods like fly swatters at a nudist's convention. Thus, if business is good, the rise is quickly reflected in the company's dividends. Obviously, you've given up a whopping amount of stability in buying such stock; if business suddenly turns sour these firms are the first to chop dividends when the bottom falls out.

When you aim for growth stocks, though, you're largely ignoring the company's immediate fortunes and are looking far ahead—some 10, 15 or 20 years ahead—during which time you are betting that the firm's expansion and modernization program will bring about a sharp increase in the stock's value. Expansion—as you may remember from the time when you decided to enlarge the basement furnace room to include an Olympic-size swimming pool—is expensive. For this reason, most so-called growth companies plow a huge part of their earnings back into the business and leave relatively little—less than 50 per cent as a general rule—to be paid out in the form of dividends.

Which is the best investment goal? It's like asking who is the prettiest of us all; out of any 10 random people, you will get at least eight different answers. Logically, if you're pushing retirement age down at the pool-cue plant or are well into a graceful middle age, your problem is that of investing in stocks that are as secure as possible. You're simply in no position to take wild flings with money that you won't have time to replace in case of loss.

Suppose you are supplementing your Social Security checks with the dividends (4 per cent) on $30,000 worth of stocks that you have purchased with the proceeds of an endowment insurance policy and the sale of your home in the wintery north. This gives you a very welcome additional income of $1,200 a year. If you go into a less stable stock just to gain another 1 per cent a year you have picked up only $300 more a year and have probably increased your risk of future slashed dividends—or outright loss of your investment, fourfold.

On the other hand, if you're one of those bright-eyed young men pictured by the magazines as an Earnest Striver with a modest income that you can hardly afford to be blasé about losing because of a house full of small, voracious mouths that need filling some 12 times a day, you should aim for stocks with a higher yield and some potential of growth. The risk is greater than that being taken by the retired couple, but a loss wouldn't be the same vital matter with you that it is with them—since you still have a job and presumably, if you keep your nose clean, a future.

If you can forego immediate income, however, and maybe don't even want it because of taxes, the answer for you is probably growth stocks. At the moment, these may be paying nothing at all in the way of dividends, or they may be paying it in the form of small stock dividends, or they may be paying up to about 2 or 2½ per cent in cash dividends, or they may be paying a combination dividend—for instance, a fractional cash dividend plus a 10 or 15 per cent stock dividend.

What you are actually gambling on in a growth company is

The "Perfect" Stock and Other Fables 37

the possibility that the company will soar in stature and wealth —in which case dividends will start getting more liberal. It makes for a sort of togetherness—you and the company growing up hand in hand. But at the same time time the big attraction in growth stock lies in the hope that increased company stature will greatly stimulate investor-demand for the stock. It will in turn multiply in value, and as the demand increases the company will find it advisable to split the stock four or five for one, both for the purpose of increasing the amount of stock available for trading and to lower the price back to where the majority of investors can afford to buy it.

Some of the best-known stocks on the market today—in the process of being growth stocks for years—have been split and re-split so many times that they look like a rail fence, and in transition they have carried a lot of those early investors along to very fat bank accounts. Ten shares of International Business Machine stock back in 1915, for instance, would have cost you $480. As of November 1958, these original 10 shares would have grown to 670 shares worth $298,688.16. Such thoughts only tend to make a healthy, red-blooded American boy greedy and should be hurriedly thrust from his mind. They are thoughts that only the very wealthy can afford.

Assuming that you have an over-all policy in mind, one that reflects your interest in the type of stock best suited for you, the next step is to lay out an investment portfolio aimed at the systematic accumulation of a well-balanced list of stocks. "Portfolio," incidentally, is a perfectly good word although it has picked up some nasty connotations implying that you have to have white-wigged foot servants and a six-figure income before you may drop remarks about "my portfolio." Actually, you've got yourself a "portfolio" if you own one share of Consolidated Tweezers.

Generally speaking, financial experts in this sort of thing arbitrarily pick a figure of about $500 as the minimum investment in any single stock. This doesn't mean that you have to have a chunk of cash this big to plop down for your whole portfolio, but an arbitrary goal of, say, $500 in each of five common stocks makes not only a neat little portfolio but also a long-range goal at which you can shoot. When you get to your goal, enlarge it to an aim of $1,000 each.

In other words you might invest $30 one month in stock A, $30 the next month in stock B, $30 the next month in stock C, and on down the line until you have approximately $500 in each.

You're aiming at diversification, of course, but it's a little silly to go overboard and end up in 10 years with something like three shares in each of 40 stocks. The principle of diversification—like sobriety—can get pretty ridiculous when carried to extremes. At the other end of the scale, so say the experts, you shouldn't wind up with more than 20 to 30 per cent of your investment in any one industry.

Since the main purpose of planning a portfolio is to protect yourself as much as possible from the unforeseeable, it is comforting to dwell on the fact that there are varying degrees of stability built into all stocks whether they are classified as income, growth or appreciative issues. This makes it possible to build up a relatively "safe" portfolio even though you make your selections from nothing but the so-called growth companies. Understandably, stocks that fall under the speculative heading are a case unto themselves and "safety" in this department is hardly apt—no speculative stock is really "safe" in the way we mean it here.

And so, Daddy Warbucks, won't you tell us what a sample growth portfolio of five stocks might look like? Well, here's a

The "Perfect" Stock and Other Fables

list of five stocks in large companies, all of which are generally classified as growth situations and each of which is in a different industry: (1) International Paper, (2) International Business Machines (still listed as a growth company, you see, even after more than forty years); (3) Aluminum Company of America, (4) Dow Chemical and (5) Amerada Petroleum.

Now let's take a look at a sample portfolio of five stocks selected for their solid-as-a-rock dependability for paying dividends. None of these, by the by, has missed a dividend in more than 50 years: (1) Kroger Company, (2) Otis Elevator, (3) Philadelphia Electric, (4) Sherwin-Williams and (5) Sterling Drug.

In between are the cyclical stocks—issues, as has been mentioned, that you might select to ride with in a bull market when they are likely to puff up abnormally in value. They aren't, you realize, stocks that you put in a lockbox and forget, since in a sudden market weakness they would be among the first to reflect rough times. Purely as an example, here are five firms generally considered cyclical in nature: (1) Boeing Airplane, (2) Chrysler Corporation, (3) Johns-Manville, (4) Zenith Radio and (5) Republic Steel.

A word of warning: a portfolio is not something you can draw up and sit on like a proud hen—even in the case of a high-security portfolio. Don't flit around re-hauling your portfolio at every jiggle of the market, but be prepared to make sensible charges when a study of the situation warrants it.

5

Heavy Stuff: The "Senior" Equities

TAKE the fancy façade off the headquarters of the International Amalgamated Cherry-Pitter Company and, aside from a lot of cherry skins, what do we find, pray?

Underneath it all—if we may be permitted to give the death-kick to a very, very tired cliché—we find that "business is people." If that isn't a precious little thought to brood over, my name isn't Jean Lafitte.

Take away the high-finance gobbledygook, and the budget and money problems of the average corporation emerge as very familiar headaches indeed. How to raise money? How to repay it? How to keep the creditors from sending nasty letters reflecting on our ancestry? Bills! Bills! Bills!

Just as most of us mere humans have monthly indebtedness to take care of in the form of mortgage payments, charge accounts, finance company payments, car payments, personal IOU's and unforgiving bookies, so—on the yacht level—does the average corporation. Neither of us can stall indefinitely, and the corporation is further handicapped by the fact that a 1,500,000-square-foot plant is hardly in a position to go hide in its sister's house at bill-paying time.

In the case of a corporation, of course, the red-ink side of the ledger usually reads something like this, only with more feeling:

First mortgage bonds (4 per cent in the amount of $10,000,000); Debentures (5 per cent in the amount of $2,000,000); Preferred stock (50,000 shares at a par value of $50 a share); and Common stock (3,000,000 shares at par $5).

While we're primarily interested in the subject of common stocks, it behooves us to take a look at these other forms of debt —both because they offer some fascinating investment possibilities under certain conditions, and because they get a whack at a company's earnings before we, as common stockholders, get our slice of the pie.

Unlike common stocks, which represent a fractional share of ownership in a corporation, bonds are simply a flat, unequivocal IOU. This gives the bondholders, naturally, a certain smug advantage over the holders of common stocks since they have a priority on any money earned by the company. If you hold a 4-per-cent bond maturing in 1967, you receive a 4-per-cent return on your money every year and, in 1967, get back your original investment—the face value of the bond.

Ownership of the bond also gives you the power to drag the company into court, sue, and possibly seize property if your payments aren't being made. It's a power that has turned many an investor's pretty head.

On the other side of the ledger, the bondholder sacrifices certain things for this sort of security. He has no voice in the operation of the company as long as his 4 per cent rolls in on schedule. Also, in a bull market such as one finds today on the stock market, the bondholder finds himself in the position of gaining nothing if Amalgamated Cherry-Pitter's common stock runs wild, doubling in price, boosting dividends and splitting all over the place. He can only brood about it.

Heavy Stuff: The "Senior" Equities

After the company has satisfied its grumpy bondholders every year, the next batch of investors standing in line with their mess kits at the "ready" position are the holders of debentures—a sort of junior-grade bond. Unlike regular bonds, which are claims against a specific plant (or in the case of railroads against a specific stretch of track), debentures are simply claims against the company's good name—assuming it has one. While all of this makes the holding of bonds and debentures look about as safe as having a private passkey to Fort Knox, it should be pointed out that both instruments are simply as sound as the company behind them—no more and no less. Having a valid claim against 1/35,000th of a falling-down plant that no longer produces marketable cherry-pitters can be a pretty hollow satisfaction.

Before the common stockholders get up to the trough there is still one more class of investor to be satisfied—the holder of preferred stocks in the corporation. Preferred stocks, like bonds, can get a bit complicated, but in general the chief characteristic is that the preferred stockholder gets his bite—usually a fixed dividend—after the holders of bonds and debentures do, but before the common stockholders shuffle up in line.

"Straight preferred" stock, as should be fairly obvious, is simply a stock on which the holder gets his stated dividend before distribution is made to common stockholders. In bad times, however, even he may find his dividends waived.

Another form of preferred stock is known as "cumulative preferred." It has the same features of straight preferred with one notable exception: in the event that dividends are waived, they must be made up sometime in the future before any common stockholder gets a dividend. Thus, in poor periods of business, these unpaid dividends pile up as a future obligation of the corporation. A very cozy little hedge, this provision makes the cumulative preferred stock sell appreciably higher than straight preferred.

Even better is a gimmick known as "convertibility," which can be tied in to both preferred stocks and to bonds. In essence, a convertible preferred stock or bond carries a proviso allowing the holder to exchange it for common stock in the company at the discretion of the investor.

Just what advantage all this has isn't one of those things that jumps immediately into your lap whistling the prelude to *Carmen*. Advantages there are, however, for both the investor and the company issuing the convertibles.

First, being a fixed-return investment, the convertible bond or preferred stock gives the investor a high degree of safety at a time in the market when things may be a bit on the unsettled side. Come what may, he'll get his before the common folk are called up for a profit tidbit.

Unlike conventional bonds, or preferred stocks, though, the convertibles have an interesting advantage that is completely alien to regular, fixed-return investment. This is the freedom that the holder of convertibles has in switching over to common stock if the market zooms up and carries the price of the common stock with it. In uncertain times the investor thus enjoys the relative security of a bond or of preferred stock, but if a bull market erupts he can join in the fun by switching to the gaiety of common-stock ownership.

This is the reason why, as the current bull market started making noises as if it was going to roar up to the ceiling, convertible preferred stock and bonds enjoyed a sudden popularity that almost put them in the category of being a fad—like wearing Bird of Paradise feathers. Because of the bobbing around of the market, investors couldn't quite decide whether the obvi-

Heavy Stuff: The "Senior" Equities

ously bullish signs were true or whether they were simply a smoke screen for an upcoming major slump in the market. To be on the safe side, ready to jump either way, investors turned to the convertibles to sweat out that critical period. As the bull market began vigorously asserting itself, conversions to common stock came thick and fast.

Roughly, then, here's how this convertibility feature works: we'll say that Bide-A-Wee Tranquilizers, Inc., issues $10,000,000 worth of convertible bonds. As bonds these pay off at the rate of 4 per cent a year until redemption in 1979. At any time you may elect to surrender each $100 bond for two shares of the company's common stock. Currently, we'll say, it's selling on the market for about $45 a share; so naturally there's no advantage in converting at the moment.

But a bull market cometh! Within a few months the price of Bide-A-Wee Tranquilizers (ticker symbol: ZZZZ) has jumped to $60 a share. And there you smugly sit, in a position to turn in one $100 bond and get back two shares of stock worth a total of $120. It's about as close as you can come in this world to that old cliché—having your cake and eating it too.

Another common arrangement allows the holder of a convertible bond or preferred stock to turn his present holdings in, plus a predetermined amount of money, and get his common stock. You might find, for example, situations where you must add, we'll say, $40 to each $100 convertible bond in order to receive one share of common stock selling on the open market at $150 a share.

One point should be emphasized concerning both convertible preferred stock and convertible bonds—they're like having your nose bobbed. Once you've made the decision to convert and have turned in your preferred stock or bond and received common stock in exchange, you can't suddenly turn around and decide to re-convert from common stock to bonds or preferred stock. To mix a very dry metaphor, having decided to cross the Rubicon you're right smack in the same boat with the rest of the common stockholders and will take your knocks like a little man in case the common stock suddenly goes sour.

Some mention should also be made here of the "participating preferred" stock—another gimmick that has as its aim the buttering of both sides of your bread. Essentially it's a straight preferred stock with all of the priority associated with that type of equity. But at the same time the "participating preferred" stock has a joker in it that cuts the preferred stockholder in for an additional share of any excess earnings in good times once the common stockholders have been taken care of—a sort of "coming back for seconds" arrangement that helps the preferred stockholder avoid the bitterness that normally comes when he sees the common stock soaring while he sits on the sidelines.

All of these devices, it should be explained, are a little on the tricky side and are normally the province of the investor who is hip. There are, however, some very valuable advantages—as well as drawbacks—in them, and there's no reason why any one group of investors should get hoggy about it. But before getting too deeply involved in preferred stocks, bonds, debentures and all of their offshoots, it would be wise to go into deep, soul-searching consultation with your broker.

6

One Foot in the Boat: Income and Growth

Once upon a time there was this dog, strolling along and whistling between his teeth. Suddenly—just like in the movies—he found a fine juicy ham hock lying in the gutter and, thinking what a lucky dog he was, snatched it up and went carrying it proudly home.

On the way, however, it was necessary to cross a low-slung toll bridge, and while stopping for a moment to admire the reflected sheen of his coat in the water he saw what seemed to be another dog with an even bigger bone in his mouth. As a matter of fact, that's exactly what it was. In the ensuing fight both dogs dropped their bones, caught terrific colds and ended up applying to Blue Cross for hospitalization.

The moral of all this is that you can't have your ham hock and eat it too.

Of all the painful and dreary lessons that one must learn this is one of the dreariest and, alas, one that investors never quite—deep down in their hearts—believe.

In investments, for instance, you have government bonds at one end of the scale and stock shares in the Little Hopeless Uranium, Silver, Gold, Platinum, Lead and Sulphur Exploration Company at the other. With one you collect $3\frac{1}{4}$ per cent interest, come peace, war, inflation, depression or anything else, short of complete collapse of the country. But that's all you'll collect. With the other investment you may wind up with a handful of stiff mattress-stuffing material, or you may wind up lighting your cigars with 10-dollar bills. But you're never going to wind up with an investment having the rocklike stability of a government bond and the potentially high yield of the uranium issue.

We've talked about growth stocks before, and for a great many people—namely, those who are young enough to forego high dividends now on the better-than-average chance of ending up with a stock in 20 years that may be worth twice, three times or 10 times its present value—this is the most logical investment course to pursue.

The question arises: can't you, by yielding a little on the safety end, and yielding a little on the growth end, come up with a compromise of some sort? Some way of having all of the ham hocks you and your beneficiaries could ever hope to have?

Maybe you're too far along in years to gamble on the growth possibilities in a 20-year investment program, but you're still young enough to hate the idea of picking a stock that's just going to sit there on its haunches—paying dividends like clockwork but never going anyplace. Well, there are indeed stocks that pretty well fit the picture of good stability and fair growth.

You will find that the so-called "rock-ribbed" stocks—the ones that have paid dividends for at least 50 years—are usually tied directly to basic consumer demands. Most often they include the better tobacco, food, drug, utility and telephone companies. Even in the most conservative of these, you'll find some elements of growth—of a sort. Since they cater directly to people, it stands to reason that they'll grow a little for the simple

One Foot in the Boat: Income and Growth

reason that the population itself is growing. But in the sense that the phrase "growth stock" is used, they're way out in Nowheresville.

To have our ham hock and meat in the soup, we should consider the possibility of digging up companies that not only fill an essential need of some sort, but—by the very character of their industry—are expanding at the same time.

It's true that such a stock will not be 100 per cent safe—none ever is—or even 98 per cent safe as American Telephone and Telegraph, to pluck an example, is considered to be. On the other hand, isn't it worth a very tiny risk to pick an issue that has a good chance of appreciating 5, 10 or as much as 20 per cent in the next few years?

Everyone has to make his own choice. You may choose stock in a company that has weathered everything the world has had to throw at it for the last 50 or 60 years. Let's say that you make 5 per cent on this stock. You'll make it today and, in all likelihood, you'll still be making 5 per cent when they prop the calla lily in your hand.

Or would you rather pick a stock that hasn't been paying dividends more than half that long, that pays you only 4 per cent today, on the chance that the company will increase its dividends twice in the next five years and show a fair-to-middlin' appreciation in price as well?

In the event the latter proposition pricks your interest, we should spend our time looking for stocks in companies that have a good record of steady dividend payment but at the same time are in industries not depending entirely for their growth on an increased birth rate. That they won't match a real red-hot growth stock is immaterial as long as their dividends show definite promise of keeping ahead of the cost of living.

Broadly speaking, then, let's take a look at three categories in which most authorities feel the characteristics of "income-growth" stocks can be found:

Public Utilities——A big favorite of the professional investors, electric utilities have been acting like growth companies for many years and give every indication of continuing in this way for many more. By 1970 it is expected that the electric utilities will have to generate three times the power they are producing today, and this means an expansion of at least 200 per cent in capacity during the next 10 years. When you get into utilities, of course, you have to bear in mind that they're tightly controlled by public service commissions which regulate rates.

A ceiling on dividends doesn't have an effect on prices, however, and most utility stocks have gained substantially in value in recent years. The main thing to keep in mind here is to pick a utility in a growth area—Florida, the Southwest, Southern California or any of the major metropolitan areas throughout the country that have demonstrated a strong growth pattern.

Personal Finance Companies——Since buying "on time" has become a national institution, it is safe to assume that the companies that back such "paper" will grow as the national gross product increases and as the number and variety of consumer products increases. In this group we have not only firms that finance the purchases of automobiles and appliances—such as C.I.T. Financial and Commercial Credit—but also the so-called "small loan" companies which also ride the coattails of the increasing national gross product. Such firms have the extra—if somewhat grim—advantage of being able to play both ends against the middle. In prosperous times they flourish because the taste for higher living standards stimulates buying on time, and in periods of recession they benefit as people borrow money

One Foot in the Boat: Income and Growth 51

to tide themselves over the rough spots. This gives the impression that *no one* ever pays them off—which is about right.

Foods——It's a little odd to find food company stocks listed here, perhaps, because food is food and, at first glance, it doesn't look like there's much growth potential in the business except as the population increases. Take a second look. Among some food companies (not all of them by any means), the research to develop new products is almost enough to put the electronics field to shame. Beatrice Foods Company, for instance, which produces dairy products chiefly, has doubled its annual sales since 1946 and has increased its net income by about 50 per cent. This is growth any way you slice it. Some of the other food companies to have at least five increases in dividends in the last 10 years are: Corn Products, General Foods, and Jewel Tea Company. In much the same way many of the food chains—Kroger, Safeway and the like—have shown strong growth characteristics that far exceed the rise in population through more efficient operations, greater outlets and an increase in their own manufacturing operations.

Unfortunately, growth-income stocks don't fall neatly into categories in most cases, so you—and your broker—will have to look around carefully for them. Choose up sides and make a game of it!

7

Luck, Pluck and Crossed Fingers: The Growth Stocks

Eeney, meeney, miney, moe...
Pick a stock, but will it grow?

O<small>N A</small> couple of occasions we've made mention of growth stocks—about how comforting to the wallet they are in most cases—and have then hurried on with utter disregard for the fact that about nine-tenths of the interest expressed these days on the subject of stocks is in the field of growth companies. One reason for this interest is that today's bull market—like all bull markets—has given everyone the itch to speculate, lightly, in stocks with a bit more glamour than is found in the "blue chip" issues. In addition the heavy emphasis on inflation makes the necessity for investing in stocks that stand a fair chance of growing in value a matter of immediate concern.

But for still another reason growth stocks are an important consideration: there have been few times—if any—in history when the economy was booming so explosively and when the possibility of picking stocks with exciting growth potentials has been greater. For example, it's been estimated that about 40 per cent of the aircraft industry's sales today are in products that weren't even in production two and a half years ago. And in 1960 about 16 per cent of the chemical industry's sales, 14 per cent of the textile sales and 7 per cent of the food and beverage sales will be products that were still on the drawing boards two years ago.

Obviously, times have to be pretty good before growth stocks can come into their own; in rough times the emphasis is on stability or on getting the highest possible return from invested funds. Of equal interest in today's economy is the fact that growth stocks—by virtue of plowing most of their earnings back into the company and paying small dividends—possess a distinctively favorable tax advantage.

If you are in a fairly high income-tax bracket now it should be a matter of small concern to you that the growth stock in which you have invested has paid a dividend of only 2.5 per cent a year because the firm has retained 80 per cent of its earnings for expansion and research. More liberal dividends at this time would simply throw you into a higher tax bracket.

Eventually, you hope, your growth company's value will have multiplied appreciably at no cost to you. When you finally sell out, the gain in value will be taxable at only half your regular rate and never more than 25 per cent. Even in the lower income-tax brackets this can work to your advantage. Let's say that your taxable income is about $2,000, of which 20 per cent goes for taxes and 80 per cent is retained. In this case 90 per cent of the profit realized from the sale of the stock, if you have held it at least six months, is retained.

If you're investing with an eye toward retirement, of course, this tax advantage becomes even more important. You will be in a lower tax bracket or, possibly, completely exempt from taxation.

The important question, then, is not whether growth stocks are a good investment, but rather what in the world they are! By what yardsticks can a company be measured to determine

Luck, Pluck and Crossed Fingers: The Growth Stocks 55

its possible development? There are, as you know, literally thousands of firms—many of them quite small and relatively unknown today—trading through the various exchanges and over the counter. To the layman they all look discouragingly alike, and yet many of them will be tomorrow's dreamboats. Still others, quite well known to everyone, can still be classified as growth companies even though they're under the management of the third-generation offspring of the founder. Still others, equally well known, are making noises like growth companies but have actually passed their peak. So which is which?

Even the experts will disagree on some details of what goes into the make-up of a stock with good growth potentials, but the following list of points for consideration embodies most of the generally accepted growth characteristics. Not many companies, of course, will rate high in all departments, but if too many holes exist, one is justified in viewing with a jaundiced eye the firm's contention that it is a true growth enterprise.

To check on the past record of any company, various financial statistical services—such as Moody's, Standard and Poor's and Fitch's—are available for your research at practically all brokerages and many banks.

There are the generally accepted characteristics of a growth company:

1. *The company is expanding faster than the national economy as a whole.* Currently the Gross National Product—which is the total value of all products and services we turn out—is increasing at the average rate of about 7 per cent a year. On this basis, then, a company's sales growth should be growing at no less than about 10 per cent a year.

2. *It has the ability to convert a substantial portion of its increased sales volume into increased net profits.* An eye-popping, year-to-year growth in sales alone means nothing unless

net profits keep pace, so there is cause for misgivings if net profits show a leveling off in spite of the sales gain.

3. *Expansions undertaken by the business are financed, largely, out of earnings.* Normally a growth company plows back between 40 and 70 per cent of its earnings into expansions —without relying, except incidentally, on outside financing.

4. *The company's stock has a relatively low yield.* This certainly doesn't mean that any company which pays low dividends is necessarily a growth situation, but it is tied in with Point 3, above. All other things being equal, a stock is considered to have growth potentials if all three of the above characteristics fit the situation and if the yield on the stock is between 2 and 5 per cent, not including stock dividends. If you get above a 5 per cent yield on a stock, it's a pretty safe bet that the company isn't retaining enough of its earnings to be engaged in any extensive expansion plans. During the explosive phases of a bull market, however, stock prices normally anticipate higher earnings and dividends and tend to "run ahead" of the actual facts. At these times an abnormal relationship between prices and both earnings and dividends frequently exists. For this reason the yields on practically all stocks will be lower than normal— for a time at least—and should be taken into account when computing this measurement.

5. *The company is actively engaged in a research program.* Just talking about how "great" research is hardly cuts the ice. Read the company's annual report and find out exactly how thoroughly management is actually pursuing research. If it's ignored or treated in vague generalities, you have pretty good evidence that the firm is letting others be the trail blazers.

6. *The company shows a willingness to make above-average expenditures on capital goods.* The development of new products obviously requires some heavy spending on new types of

machinery and plants. It's the sort of thing that can be overdone, of course, but on the whole it's pretty conclusive proof that the company is serious in following up on its research program and doesn't maintain a skeleton research staff simply as window-dressing.

7. *The company is in an industry which permits a comparatively low ratio of labor costs to total sales.* Most of the financial statistical services have broken down labor costs for each company in terms of what percentage of sales they constitute. A comparison of several representative companies in this respect will give you a pretty accurate picture of how these costs run.

Whereas too much significance shouldn't be read into labor costs alone, they make up a factor that should be reckoned in your determination of the firm's growth potential. The range of labor costs, incidentally, runs all the way from about 46 per cent of sales in shipbuilding and repairing, down to about 6 per cent in the case of tobacco processing and petroleum refining.

8. *There is relative freedom from strikes and slowdowns.* This speaks pretty well for itself—strikes and slowdowns are costly. While any company will experience an occasional work stoppage, a long history of such occurrences is fair evidence that no Merlin is going to pop out of the woodwork, wave a wand and create a 20-year period of labor-management harmony. Life is one thing, art another.

9. *The company's management has a philosophy of growth.* This subject is about as hard to handle as gelatin eaten with a salad fork. An examination of the company's annual report should give you a good idea of how management feels about this. There should be a strong emphasis on the future—not merely an attempt to appraise difficulties that the company will be expected to face in the future but a positive attitude toward enlarging its share of the market. In many annual reports, un-

fortunately, you will find more space devoted to discussions of ways and means of maintaining the company's present, satisfactory, position.

As a point of interest, the brokerage firm of Thomson and McKinnon recently asked a representative group of financial experts to submit a list of industries that each considered to be true growth situations. In 100 per cent of the replies received, chemicals, electronics and oils were listed as growth industries. In at least 70 per cent of the replies, natural gas, office equipment and paper were listed. Those industries listed by at least 50 per cent of the experts included aircraft manufacture, air conditioning, air transport, aluminum, automation, construction, containers, glass, insurance, rare metals and rubber.

Note anything significant in the lack of unanimity?

8

Russo-American Roulette: How to Speculate

Who knows? One of these days your small son may come running home from school sporting a black eye and various other open wounds, and crying his beady little eyes out.

"Daddy! Daddy!" he'll blurt out between sobs. "All the kids say that you're a . . . a . . . speculator! It isn't true, is it? Is it? Is it?"

Alas! The ancient art of speculation has indeed fallen on evil days with most of the citizenry and now ranks as just a few steps removed from active participation in the hot-car racket. If you care at all what the neighbors are saying, you defend your dabbling in the stock market by billing yourself as an "investor" or as a "trader."

And it's ironic on at least a couple of scores. There isn't a man-jack among us (nautical term) who doesn't speculate in some way every day. For instance, you may decide to buy a second-hand car now instead of later in the year because you figure that prices are lower now than they will be then—but isn't it a matter of speculation that such will be the case?

Quite apart from the fact that it's no one's business if you want to take a fling in the market, it's too often forgotten that out-and-out speculation made it possible for a lot of today's big firms to make the grade. For that matter, no one could call Queen Isabella's investment in Christopher Columbus a real "blue chip." If the day ever comes when speculation has become so disreputable—or so heavily taxed—that no one engages in it, the country's in trouble. Initial "risk" money gives birth to tomorrow's growth companies.

The principal difference between the investor and the speculator is that the former presumes himself to be salting his money away for either a nice safe income or for long-term appreciation while the speculator is out for a relatively fast turnover. To speculate successfully you must be economically and psychologically prepared to lose every fat cent you're playing with if that's the way the old ball bounces. Unfortunately, too many people who put their money into stocks are speculators by inclination but investors by temperament—a sure one-way trip to a wet restraining sheet in some quiet Happiness House.

Significantly enough, it is at times like the present that the old fire of speculative fever begins bubbling up like the sap in spring in people who ordinarily wouldn't be caught in a fixed game of penny-toss. The reason should be fairly obvious: for months we have been caught up in a turbulent market that has skyrocketed the market averages and has already lined the pockets of a lot of speculators. The feeling is strong in the air that there's still a lot more where that came from!

At such times as these you'll find speculative interest picking up sharply in at least three approaches to the market that differ considerably from the old humdrum business of picking good growth stocks and hanging on for the long haul.

Essentially, the three most popular avenues of out-and-out speculation during a bull market are (1) low-priced stocks, (2) warrants, and (3) the "put" and "call" market.

For all practical purposes, a low-priced stock is generally

Russo-American Roulette: How to Speculate

thought of as one selling for less than $20 or $25—quite frequently down as low as $2 or $4—a share. As a rule, it sells in this price bracket either because it hasn't been around long enough to have established a known record of any kind or because it is an older company in a depressed condition or industry.

Just why low-priced stocks pick up steam often out of proportion to their actual potential in a bull market is a question with fairly logical answers. In the first place a bull market naturally attracts more small investors than a stable market, and small investors tend to favor stocks selling under $25 a share more than they do the more expensive issues. Thus, the turnover in low-priced stocks accelerates sharply as a bull market expands. It's undeniably more fun to own 300 shares of stock worth $10 than to have to admit that you own only 20 shares—even though they are worth $150 apiece.

In line with this is the fact that—in a rapidly rising market a low-priced stock naturally has a better chance of showing an impressive percentage gain than does a higher priced stock. Which, for instance, has a better chance of tripling in value in the excitement of a bull market: Consolidated Cue Tips, selling at $10 a share, or International Things selling at $125 a share? Remember that Consolidated Cue Tips has only to rise ten points to double the speculator's money.

Thus, cannibal-like, the low-priced stocks feed on themselves, and in the really frantic final stages of an all-out bull market, 5-dollar-a-share stocks have been known to quadruple in value in just a few weeks.

This sounds so dandy that there must be something wrong with it. Of course there is. While low-priced stocks may do some spectacular nip-ups when the whole market is on the upswing, it should be pointed out that they are also the first to bite the dust in a bear market. The $5 stock that roars up to $20 a share with a lot of whooping, hollering and waving of flags can also plunge back to 25 cents a share in less time than it takes to say: "Show me to the window ledge."

Even as a long-term investment, a low-priced stock is naturally more of a speculation than an issue with more solidity to it; but simply because they are speculative certainly doesn't mean that there aren't still some excellent investments among them for the long haul. Most advisors recommend, though, that you shouldn't put more than 5 or 10 per cent of your available money in such stocks, and that you study the ones in which you plan to invest with the same thoroughness that you do stocks costing ten times as much.

You won't, of course. Practically no one ever does. But please don't hock the candy store to take a flyer on 5,000 shares of Amalgamated Bird Calls at $3 a share without first finding out what the birds think of the product.

Next to low-priced stocks, the second most popular speculative device in a bull market is probably that dimpled darling of Wall Street known as the "common," or "pea-under-the-walnut-shell" warrant. And what, pray, might warrants be? Basically, they are only certificates issued by a firm which give the holder, usually during some specified period of time, the right to buy common stock at a predetermined price. And, in a business where oddities are the rule rather than the exception, warrants are freaks unto themselves. A warrant is a piece of paper that gives the holder no dividends, no voting power, no claim at all on a company's earnings, and can become completely worthless overnight. Good grief! What makes them of value under any set of circumstances?

Well, let's say that you buy 1,000 warrants issued by the Consolidated Lint, Dross and Flotsam Company giving you the right to buy 1,000 shares of the company's stock at $15 a share. The stock is currently selling at exactly $15.25 a share, which at the moment makes the warrants—mathematically, at least—worth 25 cents apiece. It hardly sounds like the sort of thing you can go around pricing yachts on, since you would simply break even if you paid 25 cents to buy a document that entitles you to pay only $15 for a share of stock now selling at $15.25.

Here, though, is where the attraction of warrants comes to the fore: suppose the price of the common stock of CLD&F suddenly soars and bobs around at $45 a share? And there you sit with a little piece of paper entitling you to buy 1,000 shares at only $15 a share. This makes each warrant worth not the 25 cents you paid for it but a cool $29.75 apiece.

Now you could go to the bank and borrow $15,000. (Don't worry! They'd lend it to you!) You would exercise the warrant and buy 1,000 shares of the common stock at your guaranteed price of $15 apiece ($15,000). Then you turn right around, sell the stock at the market price of $45,000, repay your $15,000 bank note, and pocket a clear $15,000—less commissions—on an investment of only $250. Unlikely? It usually is, but before we laugh it off as a big joke and go back to currying the goats, let's look at a classic case.

Back in 1942, RKO issued warrants that sold on the market for 6¼ cents apiece. Just four years later the warrants alone were selling for $13 apiece and $500 invested in them in 1942 would have returned $104,000 a paltry four years later. For sheer speculative glamour there probably hasn't been anything like common stock warrants since they gave up trying to make gold out of lizards' tongues.

Two things at least work in the distinct favor of warrants from the glamour standpoint: (1) In relation to the price of the firm's common stock they're dirt cheap. Why shouldn't they be? No dividends, no privileges and a huge risk. (2) The market in warrants themselves tends to make the fluctuating price for a warrant follow almost exactly the pattern of the common stock to which it is related. Theoretically you can buy warrants and share in a company's fortunes with only a fraction of the cash you would need to buy its common stock. This is the interesting economic principle known as "leverage."

Having inflated this nice bubble known as warrants, we will now stick pins in it by pointing out that these certificates also have a couple of staggering drawbacks leading to possible bankruptcy and all that mess.

Since warrants are pegged at a specific, predetermined price at which they entitle you to buy the actual stock, it stands to reason that the bottom can fall out of them faster than it could out of a sugar boat. The same CLD&F warrants allowing you to buy the common stock at $15 a share, which we mentioned earlier, obviously have a value only as long as the price of the common stays above $15 a share. In a sudden market decline the price of the common stock could easily sink to $5 a share and stay there indefinitely—in which case your fertile imagination should provide you with the answer to the question of what the warrants would then be worth! Scratch pads, anyone?

There is still another little joker in common stock warrants that adds a particular spice to this form of speculation. A great many of the warrants issued have specific time limits on them, thus catching you in a double squeeze play. Not only are you gambling that the common stock will increase enough to give your warrants some value, but you're also gambling that this happy turn of affairs will happen before the warrants expire. Think how awkward it would be to have on Monday a sockful of warrants due to expire at the end of the week with the price of the common stock still hovering about $10 a share under the level at which the warrants would be any good. Ah, hah! What a big joke on you—and your widow!

"Perpetual" issues, on the other hand, have no time limit on them at all—an advantage, naturally, but still no guarantee that they won't sink in value down to zero and stay there for the next 50 years.

Why does a company issue such an oddball gimmick in the first place? Well, quite frankly, it's most often nothing but a sweetener to accompany a new stock issue that the firm fears—usually with ample justification—will go over with investors like a case of hives.

It's interesting to note here that $25,000 spent on Universal Picture warrants (selling at $39 apiece) in 1945 had shrunk to only $750 just two years later as the warrants dwindled in value to $1.50 apiece. This made for a million laughs in some circles, as you can imagine.

In at least one respect, that of contracting in future promises, warrants have something in common with the interesting "put" and "call" market. Stripped of its Monopoly-type language, the put and call market is nothing but the buying of options to buy or sell stock at some future date.

In actual practice they are exactly the same sort of bargain you strike when you suspect there's oil on a farmer's land and you agree to pay a $200 option to buy the land in sixty days at $3,000 an acre. If your test drillings indicate the presence of oil, you congratulate yourself on having been such a shrewd fellow. If the property turns out to have less oil in it than your crankcase, you're out only $200. The speculative aspects of puts and calls is admitted more freely by Wall Street than virtually any other trading device, and periodically some bluenose is trying to get the whole procedure outlawed.

On the stock market, put and call options work this way: Say United Wren Houses is selling at $35 a share and you're fully convinced that the price is due to rise to at least $50 or $55 before the end of the year. You don't feel strongly enough about it to risk the $3,500 that would be necessary to buy 100 shares of it, but you still feel that it's definite enough to risk a little money.

At this point you go to your broker (who works on such matters through a special put-and-call broker who underwrites these deals) and buy a "call" on United Wren Houses for, we'll say, between 400 and 500 dollars. This means that any time within the length of the option—30, 60, 90 or 180 days, whichever it is you've bought—you can turn in your option contract to the broker and demand that he sell you 100 shares of United Wren at $35 a share.

If you've guessed right you are able to plank down $3,500 for the stock, then turn around and sell it at the higher market price. If it went up to $50, as you hoped, you've made a $1,500 profit—less the $450 you spent on the call and on commissions. If you've guessed wrong and the stock is down in the neighborhood of $30 a share, it would be silly of you to exercise the option so you simply swallow the $450 loss like a big boy and go home and beat your wife.

A "put"—as you might have guessed—is just the opposite. In this case you think that United Wren Houses is going to go down, but you don't feel confident enough about it to put up the amount of money required for a "short" sale. Instead, you buy a put from your broker. This means that at any time within the life of the option you can present the put to the broker and compel him to buy from you 100 shares of the stock at the market price prevailing when you bought the option.

Thus, if you bought the put when United Wren Houses was

selling for $35, you can wait until it has slipped to $25 and then buy 100 shares of it on the market. You take these to your broker with your put and he is obligated to buy them from you at the old price of $35.

What puts and calls will cost you depend greatly on the price of the stock on the market, its record of stability and the length of the option. A 180-day put or call on a high-priced stock that has a record of wild jumpiness in the market is obviously going to cost you a whale of a lot more than a 30-day put or call on a low-priced, stable issue.

While chiefly a speculative device, both puts and calls are frequently used by professionals as a form of insurance. An investor with a huge profit, for instance, will often buy a put at the high market price simply to protect himself against a declining market for the next few months. If the decline he fears doesn't occur, he is still inclined to view the put fee as money well spent since it served its purpose of acting as an insurance policy for him.

Whether all of these forms of speculation are "moral" or not, is a question in someone else's realm. One thing is certain: they're trickier than making a chip shot with a bent curtain rod.

9

Rocks of Ages: The Blue Chips

THERE comes a time in any well-regulated life when the old zest for playing skin-the-cat on pear trees becomes of less pressing urgency. A bit silly, even.

And, in investments, too, there comes a time in life when the *whee-di-dee* approaches to the subject—the speculations, the "businessmen's risks," and the long-term growth situations—are no longer the answer. With age one begins thinking somewhat less about growth stocks that may develop into real moneymakers in another 10 or 15 years and thinks instead about stocks with considerably less "dash" but far more security. At this point you are probably quite gray at the temples.

At the age of 30 or 40 a calculated risk is of course quite in order. You can afford to sacrifice a little in safety and quite a bit more in dividends if the stock you have settled on shows concrete indications of future growth. You can afford this risk because you're still gainfully employed and presumably have quite a few more years of productivity ahead of you. So the stock goes poof? With a gay little laugh and four hookers of straight rye you bend back to the task of recouping your losses, which, fortunately, you have time to do before they truss you up and haul you off to the restful home with the wide veranda.

Comes age 65, the engraved watch from the usual office shake-down, and the Florida cottage. Getting cute with your investments slips into the category of silliness. Naturally you want as handsome a dividend as you can get, but you want it with the nearest thing to absolute safety that you can find.

Let us say that you have retired on your Social Security income and a supplemental pension which you and your employer have been jointly kicking into these many years. On top of this, you have $15,000 in cash savings. You can invest this money—we'll say—in rock-ribbed stocks paying an average of 4½ per cent in dividends every year. This puts $675 additional spending money in your pocket—$56.25 a month. It isn't enough for a wild succession of champagne parties, but it can buy an impressive number of little conveniences and luxuries on the normal person's retirement scale of living that might not otherwise be possible.

Suppose, though, that you fall for the siren songs filling the air these days with more regularity than rock 'n' roll? You trot down to your broker and put your $15,000 in stocks on which the average dividend is 7 per cent a year—cyclical stuff in an industry that is at the moment cutting all sorts of production and sales records. This boosts your annual income from this source to $1,050 or $87.50 a month—a 45 per cent "improvement."

It stands to reason that the risk inherent in a stock consistently paying 7 per cent a year ("consistent," that is, in that it looks as if that's what it'll be paying in the future) is going to be considerably greater than in one paying 4½ per cent. And the increase in risk may not be a 45 per cent increase—it may well be a 400 per cent increase. (There are a few exceptions, but generally speaking the fatness of the dividend is usually in direct proportion to the risk.)

Rocks of Ages: The Blue Chips

One needn't go back in history any farther than the final quarter of 1957—in the middle of the so-called "Sputnik Recession"—for examples of what happens to cyclical stocks when the bottom temporarily drops out from under. Penn-Dixie stockholders, for example, found themselves dividend-less at the end of the third quarter of that year, and in the next quarter things had deteriorated to the point where the preferred stockholders, too, were denied a quarterly payment. Grumman Aircraft and Baltimore and Ohio Railroad were only two of a long list of companies that cut their dividends in half. And in even worse condition were stockholders of Bigelow-Sanford and Loew's—to name only two of another distressingly long list—who also omitted a fourth-quarter dividend.

The question that must be faced squarely is this: Is it more desirable to be able to count on a sure $56.25 a month during those graceful years of retirement, or is it worth an extra $41.25 a month even if you know full well that there may be nothing at all coming in from your investments for long months at a time? It's a decision that no one can make for you—to take $56.25 for sure, or to take $87.50 maybe.

There is no such thing as 100 per cent "safe" stock any more than there is a 100 per cent "safe" way to walk across the street during rush hour. But there are, indeed, many, many stocks on the market that have paid dividends for decade after decade—through wars, depressions, locust plagues and virtually every other blight known to civilization. While it doesn't mean that they couldn't run into trouble in some future year, these stocks are—for all practical purposes—as "safe" as one can get and still be involved in the stock market.

Here, for example, is a partial list of stocks found on the major exchanges that have paid dividends in cash each year for at least 50 years. Some have paid for more than 100 years. The figure in parentheses refers to the year in which the firm's payment of uninterrupted cash dividends began:

Acme Steel (1901)
Amer. Elec. Pwr. (1909)
Amer. Natl. Gas (1904)
Amer. Snuff (1903)
Amer. Tobacco (1905)
Bell Tel. of Canada (1881)
Boston Edison (1890)
Brit. Amer. Oil (1909)
Campbell Soup (1902)
Carpenter Steel (1907)
Cent. Hudson Gas & Elec. (1903)
Chesebrough-Pond's (1883)
Coca-Cola (1893)
Commonwealth Edison (1890)
Continental Ins. (1853)
Detroit Edison (1909)
Draper Corp. (1897)
Eastman Kodak (1902)
Fairmount Foods (1905)
General Cigar (1909)
General Mills (1898)
W. T. Grant Co. (1907)
Hartford Elec. Light (1901)
Imperial Oil Ltd. (1890)
Johnson & Johnson (1905)
Link-Belt Co. (1875)
National Biscuit (1899)

Allied Chemical (1887)
Amer. Hardware (1902)
Amer. News (1864)
Amer. Tel. & Tel. (1881)
Beech-Nut Life Savers (1902)
Borden Co. (1899)
Bristol-Myers (1900)
Burroughs Corp. (1895)
Cannon Mills (1890)
Carter Products (1883)
Chain Belt (1894)
Cincinnati Gas & Elec. (1853)
Colgate-Palmolive (1895)
Cons. Edison of NY (1885)
Corning Glass (1881)
Diamond Gardner (1882)
DuPont (1904)
Elect. Stor. Battery (1901)
Fid.-Penix Fire Ins. (1889)
General Elec. (1899)
Goodman Mfg. (1900)
Hackensack Water (1886)
Hecla Mining (1903)
Ins. Co. of N. Amer. (1875)
Kroger Co. (1902)
MacAndrews & Forbes (1903)

Rocks of Ages: The Blue Chips

National Lead (1906)
N. J. Zinc (1882)
Norfolk & Western (1901)
Parke, Davis & Co. (1878)
Pennsylvania R. R. (1848)
Chas. Pfizer (1901)
Pitts. & Lake Erie (1886)
Potomac Elec. Power (1904)
Publ. Sv. of Colo. (1907)
Pullman, Inc. (1867)
Raybestos-Manhat. (1895)
Riegel Paper (1891)
San Diego Gas & Elec. (1909)
Scovill Mfg. (1856)
Shell Trspt. & Trd. (1898)
Singer Mfg. (1863)
So. Cal. Edison (1907)
Std. Oil of Ind. (1894)
Sterling Drugs (1902)
Tampa Elec. (1900)
Union Elec. Co. (1906)
United Engineering (1902)
United Gas Impr. (1885)
U. S. Playing Card (1896)
Wash. Gas. Lt. (1852)
W. Va. Pulp & Paper (1892)
White Dental (1881)

Natl. Fuel Gas (1903)
N. J. Tel. & Tel. (1886)
N. Y. Hond. Rosario (1896)
Pacific Lighting (1909)
Pennsalt Chemicals (1863)
Pepperell Mfg. (1852)
Philadelphia Elec. (1902)
Pitts. Plate Glass (1899)
Procter & Gamble (1891)
Publ. Sv. Elec. & Gas (1907)
Quaker Oats (1906)
Reading Co. (1905)
Ruberoid Co. (1899)
Scotten Dillon (1903)
Shawinigan Water & Pwr. (1907)
Sherwin-Williams (1885)
Socony Mobil Oil (1902)
Standard Brands (1899)
Std. Oil of N. J. (1899)
Sun Oil Co. (1904)
Torrington Co. (1899)
Union Pacific R. R. (1900)
United Shoe Mach. (1905)
Upjohn Co. (1909)
Wash. Water & Pwr. (1899)
Westinghouse Air Brakes (1875)
Yale & Towne Mfg. (1899)

As exemplary as the records of such stocks are, practically all of them at one time or another have had to cut dividends at least slightly. But in most cases such reductions have come during depressions when the larger purchasing power of the dollar has in some measure offset the dividend reduction.

So even here there is nothing actually foolproof, but there's something comfortable about being both old and successful as these companies are. Many secure people have grown old right along with them. The retirement years pose enough problems under the best of circumstances, so the less fussing and fretting you have to do over the safety of your investments puts you just that much farther ahead of the game.

10

"Togetherness": Mutual Funds

"To BE quite frank about it, I wouldn't recognize a good stock investment if it jumped into my lap, draped oak leaves over my ears and planted wild kisses on my forehead!"

Or, as a variation on a theme: "Good grief! There are about 3,500 companies with stock listed on all the exchanges! How do I know what to buy? Do I tack the financial page on the wall and throw darts at it?"

There's a lot of glib talk floating around about being sure to pick the stock that "fits your needs"—a very pretty little statement that makes the whole thing sound about as complicated as choosing a Christmas card imprint. It's really the awesomeness of having to pick one or two or three stocks out of the confusing welter of available issues that probably keeps as many people away from the stock market as the lack of money—well, almost as many.

Confusing things even more for the small investor is the frequent admonition that he shouldn't "put all his eggs in one basket." He should remain "fully diversified in growth, income and stable" stock issues. Everyone seems to be a bit vague on just how a little trick like this is achieved on an investment program of $20 to $40 a month, however—it's like trying to split one pat of butter among eight crackers.

It can be done if you put a little thought in the matter and settle on periodic but regular investments in two or three widely diversified issues, as is so often done by investment-plan participants. At best, it's a fairly worrisome matter—one in which hundreds of thousands of small investors don't care to become involved.

It explains the rather extraordinary growth of the investment trusts, a gimmick born in 1924 with the formation of the Massachusetts Investors Trust but having its big boom since 1940. Today there are nearly 225 such companies in the country and they control a staggering $10,000,000,000 in their clients' acounts.

Essentially an investment trust is a company that collects money from member-shareholders and invests such funds in a wide selection of carefully chosen securities. In other words, a group of men who must be presumed to know what they are doing take on the responsibility of handling the investment programs of thousands of small and large investors who can't, or don't care to, take on the burden themselves.

So what's the advantage? They're doing nothing that a fairly smart investor couldn't do for himself. This is very true, but it's ironically the principal selling point that the investment trusts have to offer—the really shrewd investor is a rarity, but you the layman can invest through investment trusts and reap the same benefits enjoyed by him. At least, so goes the logic of the suave investment salesman with the two-hundred dollar briefcase and the ever-fresh carnation in his buttonhole.

As a member-shareholder of an investment trust you share in the assets and earnings of the trust in proportion to the amount of money you have invested with it. Its dividends to you are based on the average dividend income that it, in turn, receives from the thousands and thousands of shares of stocks that it

"Togetherness": Mutual Funds

holds in hundreds of corporations. It's like pooling your money to buy a giant-sized bag of jelly beans.

Here—at a cost of anywhere from $2 to $30 or $40 a share—the small investor can put his money in maybe 30 speculative stocks, 15 or 20 stable stocks and possibly two or three bond issues at one fell swoop. It is—as even the investment funds' foes will admit—the only way in which a small investor can spread his money over so many stock issues that it would take a national revolution, literally, to wipe him out.

As an example, let's say that you have bought a fifty-dollar share in such a fund. By this device, we'll say that you have just bought 1/1,000,000th of the assets of a company having $50,000,000 outstanding in stocks and bonds. Let's say that over the first year your fund collects $2,500,000 in dividends. Obviously your 1,000,000th share of the fund has netted $2.50 —or a return of 5 per cent. All of this, you realize, is an oversimplification of a financial situation that probably has the late J. P. Morgan spinning in his grave, but it at least illustrates the principle.

This sort of thing is known as the "open-end" type investment trust, by far the more popular of the two types now getting so much publicity, and it is simply a firm that sells shares in itself in whatever quantity it can manage to attract buyers. There's no limit on either the number of outstanding shares or on the number of shareholders. You buy in, and out, of an "open-end" investment trust whenever you want to, and the value of the shares varies in accordance with this traffic and the total value of the securities held by the firm.

To go back to the one fifty-dollar share you bought, it takes no great mathematical know-how to realize that if you had bought the same share a couple of years earlier when the fund was worth only $35,000,000, and had only 350,000 shares outstanding, your share would have cost you $100, instead of $50, because you would have been buying a proportionately larger hunk of the fund's assets.

This price-redemption ratio is watched carefully. Some investment funds, as a matter of fact, compute it daily, and some twice daily.

"Closed-end trusts," on the other hand, operate on the same principle of the "open-end trust," but their shares are bought and sold in exactly the same way that any stock company's shares are traded. They have a certain number of shares outstanding and that, period, is it. This is in direct opposition to the "open-end trusts," who promote and sell as many new shares as they can find buyers for.

Unlike closed-end trusts, which are bought and sold on standard brokerage commissions, open-end trusts charge a fee —and it varies sharply from fund to fund—for the management service that it provides in handling your money. These fees, frankly, are normally larger than the brokerage fees that you would pay if you were making up your own list of investments, but it should be borne in mind that while your own broker simply acts as an agent, doing your buying and selling for you, the investment trust has a lot of expensive talent on its payroll to keep track of the whole complex securities field. The talent of knowing what you're doing comes high—whether in the investment field or in installing plumbing.

In spite of the things that have been said here about diversification, the zooming popularity of the investment funds has brought about a situation where there is far more flexibility in choosing a fund to fit your own ideas of investment than you would think possible. Like stocks themselves, there is now a mutual fund (the popular name for open-end trusts) to suit just

"Togetherness": Mutual Funds

about every investor's taste. As a matter of fact, it's almost as difficult to pick a mutual fund now as it is to pick common stocks. You could almost say that the situation is beginning to defeat one of its own reasons for being.

Basically, the investment trusts fall loosely into just about the same four categories that stocks do:

Bond funds. These are the most conservative trusts. Most of their capital is invested in high grade mortgages and pays a relatively low dividend. They come as close to being "worry-free" as you can get in the investment field.

Balanced funds. These keep possibly 30 to 40 per cent of their capital invested in bonds or preferred stock (the rest is in common stocks) and pay a dividend slightly higher than the bond funds.

Income funds. These funds are dedicated to investments in securities paying the highest possible dividends consistent with safety and good sense. Naturally, they not only pay somewhat more than a balanced fund but are slightly riskier too.

Capital-growth funds. These funds invest chiefly in the common stock of "growth" companies—firms that plow most of their earnings back into expansion programs and may be worth far more on the market in ten years than they are today. Because growth companies are spending most of their money in a calculated risk on the future, there is relatively little left for dividends. The capital-growth funds reflect this in their own dividends, of course.

Another group of smaller investment trusts concern themselves exclusively with specific industries—electronics, utilities and even uranium—and are fine for those investors who have a "fix" on or an obsession with one branch of our economy.

Even in the "riskiest" of the mutual funds (which, of the four categories mentioned, would be the capital-growth funds), the risk is far less than it would be if you tried to pick five or six growth stocks yourself. Not every stock chosen by the fund will be successful, but through the group's diversification among many growing companies an impressive "cushion" is maintained.

All of this may seem to imply that the investment trusts are foolproof and eternally profitable, but, alas, such is not the case. True enough, you've protected yourself against disastrous drops that may be incurred by any two or three speculative stocks overnight, but it should be pointed out that you've also insulated yourself against spectacular rises in other issues. So, for the sake of protection, you've also knocked yourself out of any real hope of making a killing on the market. The question is, just how much does this sort of thing bother you?

In this same direction, investment in one of the funds mentioned doesn't spare you from possible loss if the whole market takes a down-turn. You're dealing in averages, remember, and a general drop could lower the value of every issue in your investment fund's portfolio in spite of the wide diversification. If you're forced, for some personal reason, to sell your holdings during such a depressed period—well, that's the way the chip splinters.

Probably the biggest real hazard in investment trusts at the moment lies in their awesome popularity. You will be, if you haven't already been, battered half to death by salesmen. There will be pretty brochures, impressive charts, a running patter of exciting statistics and everything short of trained seals to get your name on the dotted line. You can easily end up not knowing what in the world you've bought—except that you'll be under the vague impression that you've bought a mutual fund of some kind.

Don't be bullied. Make the salesman pin it down definitely as to whether his company adheres to a policy of conservative holdings, balanced holdings, income issues or growth situations. And then, by all means, check up even further by consulting your broker and by doing a little basic research in some source such as *Barron Weekly's* "Quarterly Mutual Fund Record" which reports each company's net asset value per share, dividends from income and disbursements from capital gains for the last 10 years (if the company's that old). Your business library will undoubtedly have this periodic survey on its shelves.

11

A Place on "The Big Board"

EVENTUALLY there comes the nagging question of why in the name of Paddy's pig any firm wants to be listed on a major stock exchange in the first place. Is it a big social advantage down at the tavern? ("I want you to meet Charlie Clegsteigel—he's listed, you know!") Does your wife like you any better for it? Do children stop stoning you in the street?

The fact that a firm wants to be listed on a major stock exchange is one of those little idiosyncrasies of business life that, at first blush, seems to be so basic as to make the question ridiculous. Actually, it's a very good question because getting your firm listed can be a real pain in the neck. You have to submit to a "physical" of your corporation structure that makes anything the Army does to inductees look like a casual glance in comparison; you have to follow strict rules of conduct that sound like recreation-yard prohibitions at a state industrial school; and, with your stock available to every nut who wants to buy it, you can end up with more crackpots at your annual meetings (who have to be treated nicely) than are attracted to the average big city bomb scare.

A number of very large firms whose names are household words have never bothered to get themselves listed on a major stock exchange. Among these are the pharmaceutical giant Eli Lilly and Company, Time, Inc., Dun and Bradstreet, and Dictaphone. There are hundreds of others. It isn't snobbishness that prompts this; the companies simply have no need of the peculiar advantages that a listing offers.

To see why and how a listing comes about on the New York Stock Exchange (which alone accounts for about 85 per cent, dollarwise, of all stock traded in the United States on all exchanges), let's take a hypothetical case—that of a Midwestern manufacturer who took over his father's olive fork factory in the early 1930s. Back in the 1890s, of course, the manufacturer's father started the small factory—the Dainty Thrust Fork Company—on $10,000 that he borrowed from a few friends.

Things went along quietly for many years until Prohibition, when the resultant speak-easies created a fresh new demand for dainty forks used in conveying olives to coffee-cup martinis. It became necessary to expand the company's plant, but with higher prices prevailing such a move meant spending about $100,000. The firm, prosperous or not, simply didn't have the money and it was obviously too much to raise through friends. After viewing the matter from all sides, the company decided to incorporate and get authorization to float a purely local stock issue—1,200 shares to be sold at $100 a share, enough to raise the required $100,000 plus expenses connected with the corporation and the selling of the stock.

And so it went for many years. Periodic expansions and modernizations were financed either internally or, when that was impossible, by getting authorization for new stock issues. The company branched out. It acquired a glass plant and turned out a line of dinnerware and tavern-style drinking glasses and picked up a run-down plant that formerly manufactured commercial and institutional dining-room furniture. The company began to require a few hundred thousand dollars here, a few hundred thousand there. And, finally, a million here and there.

Business—unfortunately or fortunately, however you want

to look at it—was too good. Orders were lost because of slow delivery dates, and labor costs ran to excessive figures because the only way to use the cramped manufacturing facilities was by resorting to two and even three shifts a day involving heavy overtime. Machinery, pushed constantly beyond its capacity, was breaking down faster.

The old days of expanding with only one or two million dollars, however, were over; the Dainty Thrust Fork Company—since changed to Dainty Thrust Enterprises—was Big Time now. Expansion on the scale needed would now take at least $15,000,000.

Now the problem is, how in the blue-eyed world do you raise a whopping amount of money like that in such a limited geographical area? It may be possible, but the time and cost of such an ambitious program is a pretty exhausting proposition. It becomes abundantly clear that Dainty Thrust Enterprises needs a nation-wide market place where its stock may be traded freely and where it will attract the attention of investors all over the country instead of in one small region. North Hamstrung is a nice town and all that, but there isn't really enough loose cash floating around in it to underwrite a good cake sale.

And so application is made for listing on the New York Stock Exchange. This simple act unleashes the same sort of official curiosity about Dainty Thrust Enterprises that would be encountered if a bearded man with a Russian accent were to apply to the State Department for a job as diplomatic courier in West Berlin.

Every company seeking listing on the New York Stock Exchange is judged on its own merits, but generally speaking the NYSE's Board of Governors first wants to know: (1) the degree of national interest in the company, (2) its relative position and stability in the industry, and (3) whether it is engaged in an expanding industry with prospects of at least maintaining its relative position.

On the bookkeeping end of all this, the NYSE normally requires that a company seeking listing on the Big Board:

1. Should have demonstrated earning power under competitive conditions of $1,000,000 annually, after all charges and taxes.

2. Should have net tangible assets of at least $8,000,000, but greater emphasis is placed on the aggregate market value of the firm's common stock where $8,000,000 at the time of listing is looked for.

3. Is expected to have at least 400,000 common shares outstanding (exclusive of concentrated or family holdings) among not less than 1,500 shareholders after substantially discounting odd lots.

4. Must be a going concern, or be the successor to a going concern.

You'll notice that the Board of Governors doesn't try to tackle the impossible job of deciding whether or not the applicant is going to set the world on fire with success once it has been listed on the Exchange. Past performance is vital in deciding what the company's chances are of growing, but no one is all-seeing in matters of this sort. You can, after all, protect potential investors only so far, and it's not exactly unknown for a corporation with 90 years of success behind it to be suddenly struck down with everything from a new line of lousy products to a multimillion-dollar theft from the company's funds by the president's son-in-law.

Assuming that Dainty Thrust Enterprises passes all the tests with flying colors, the Board of Governors gives its blessing and a nervous president of old DTE poses for a publicity photograph on the floor of the Exchange on the first day that the stock goes on the Big Board. The photographer will, of course, catch his wrong profile and he'll end up in the newspapers looking like a mailbox thief brought to bay, but that's publicity for you. The little company that began on $10,000 of borrowed capital back in the 1890s is now traveling in fast company.

In all, it's been estimated that about 800,000 U.S. corporations are currently doing business here and abroad and of these only about 1,200 are listed on the NYSE. It is, though, a pretty select group that, among them, accounts for about 13,000,000 employees—about one out of five of all civilian workers in the country. Their assets in 1956 (the last year for which complete figures are available) totaled more than $245,000,000,000 or 30 per cent of the total capital invested by private business in this country. Their revenues amounted in that same year to about $225,000,000,000, or 35 per cent of all corporate sales, and in 16 of the 27 industries for which data were available, the companies listed on the Big Board accounted for more than 50 per cent of the business activity concentrated in those industries.

By getting itself listed on the NYSE, of course, Dainty Thrust Enterprises doesn't necessarily have all of its capitalization problems automatically solved, but it's in a whale of a lot better position to raise money than it ever was before. About 655 member firms of the NYSE, for instance, have suddenly become interested in DTE, have started studying its background and its future potential and have begun trading in its stock.

DTE is no longer hamstrung by the necessity of making personal contact every time a capitalization program is required; its stock and bond issues are quickly snapped up throughout the country by thousands of investors. Everyone is happy—DTE gets the funds it needs for expansion and modernizations, and the investors get themselves a slice of an old but growing company.

12

Party! Party! The Investment Clubs

AND so there you are, ten men in a leaky lifeboat fleeing from a sinking ship. Four sharks leisurely follow and a giant manta ray lazily slaps at the keel. What course of action to follow?

Naturally you form a club, call yourself The Happy Flounderers Boating Society, elect officers and name a committee for the club's first spring dance—depending, of course, on ultimate rescue.

It's a peculiarity of the average American that he'll help form a new social club as fast as a Frenchman will help form a new coalition government cabinet. At long last, the club instinct has found a form of expression that makes immeasurably more sense than—alas!—the majority of our social and semisocial clubs. Happily too, the project, known rather loosely as "investment clubs," is going great guns and now encompasses about 15,000 groups throughout the country. And no movement in recent history has even been in a better position to avoid the stigma of being called a Communist-front group—they're so capitalistic in makeup that in comparison the National Association of Manufacturers looks pinko.

Contrary to popular belief, the investment club isn't a particularly new idea. Informal groups of investors have been pooling their resources to buy well-rounded portfolios of common stocks for a long time. As a semisocial club arrangement, the true birth of the investment club can be traced to 1940 when a group in Detroit set up an organization along lines that are still followed by most clubs. Nothing much happened to the investment club idea until about six or seven years ago when it suddenly caught fire—largely in spite of the indifference of most brokerage houses who considered it far more trouble than it was worth.

Since, I presume, there are the usual number of cynics among us, the question comes to mind: What can a broker hope to gain by wet-nursing a bunch of club members through the time-consuming business of organizing a club, setting up books, advising them, attending some of their meetings and quieting their misgivings every time the market hiccoughs? Assuming that the members of a club pool $10 apiece a month, this means that the club buys about $200 worth of stocks a month through its adviser-broker. The broker's commission is about $6—hardly enough to justify all the trouble he goes to in advising them. Why does he bother then? Can he get a merit badge for this sort of thing?

From the broker's standpoint there are several distinct advantages in being hooked up with the investment club movement. For one thing, it is an educational device aimed at acquainting people with the business of investing in stocks. The more people who get this knowledge, the more the broker will profit in the long run. In the second place, it is excellent word-of-mouth advertising for the brokerage. In the third place, many club members begin buying additional stocks, independently of the club but based on what they've learned through the club's operations. Naturally, they turn to the same broker who's been handling their club account. If they don't, of course, the broker

Party! Party! The Investment Clubs

is justified in inventing some new four-letter words to cover such ingratitude.

Finally, it's a long-range proposition from the broker's point of view. In 10 or 15 years the young junior clerk who is today all wrapped up in investing his $10 a month may be president of the company with money squirting out of his ears like a statue in a park fountain. With his considerable wealth he still returns to the brokerage house that was so patient with him in the days when $10 was half of the washing machine payment and not to be taken lightly.

Basically, the club idea is simply a gay way of studying the stock market each month with a few compatible friends and pooling a predetermined amount of money in common stocks. Dividends, stock splits and other income are all lumped together and each member is credited with his proportionate share of the "kitty."

Granted that the idea is an excellent one for all concerned, how do you get the ball rolling? It should be recognized that it's far easier—from a bookkeeping standpoint—to round up some friends and start a club from scratch than it is to join one already in operation. Here is the procedure:

1. The idea for the club will probably spring from a nucleus of two or three friends, neighbors, or people engaged in the same kind of work. This similarity of interests is very desirable although some clubs operate just as successfully on the theory that a more well-rounded club develops when the members are chosen for their variety of occupations and backgrounds. It's a matter of personal choice.

The ideal size for a club is considered to be 15 members, and, for Heaven's sake, no matter what other qualifications you look for in each other, please make sure that you'll be relatively compatible. Nothing gives a club a black name like having to call in the city riot squad from time to time. Also, from a practical standpoint, it definitely is a good idea to line up at least one member with some accounting experience—things can get pretty hilarious, if chaotic, in clubs where everyone's education in mathematics ended with a rather spotty knowledge of long division.

Brokers who have been active in setting up investment clubs advise that it isn't a good idea to pick a member who has had considerable experience in the investment field. Since most of the members of the club will be inexperienced in investment matters—and since the chief goal is one of mutual education—there is a tendency to lean too heavily on a member with some experience in the field. As a result—consciously or unconsciously—the club may turn into a rather boring parlor game of follow-the-leader.

2. The second step is for the fledgling club to get together for an organizational meeting (good excuse for a party). A name is chosen such as "The Marshbog Avenue Investment Club," "The Hole-in-the-Head Plungers," or about anything else that comes to mind. It's not a bad idea to get in touch with a broker beforehand and make sure that you're not duplicating the name of a club in the same area—it can get pretty confusing. At the same time you can pick up from him a sample of the model by-laws suggested by the National Association of Investment Clubs and invite him to the meeting. In this way he'll be on hand to answer the innumerable questions that you will have. And don't worry if the questions you drop in his lap sound a little stupid; he's heard them all and will be diplomatic enough not to look amused.

At this same organizational meeting you elect: a chairman, preferably someone who has had some experience in conducting meetings; a vice-chairman, upon whose shoulders falls the re-

Party! Party! The Investment Clubs

sponsibility of appointing investigating committee and assigning industries to be studied; a secretary, who does what secretaries always do; and an "accounting member" who is charged with the dual job of preparing a monthly "liquidating value" statement as of the last trading of the month, and of operating the club's bank and brokerage accounts. (Ah, hah! Now you see why you need somebody in the club who can accurately add up a handful of pocket change without getting the intellectual bends!)

At this meeting (I don't know whether you're going to have much time for a party, after all) you should discuss and agree on your by-laws, select a monthly meeting date and time, and determine the size of the monthly payments. These payments should be kept nominal—around $10 a month a member—so that the prime goal, education, isn't obscured.

Naturally, you can't really get into business as a club until you sign a standard "club-broker agreement" form. This contains the signature of everyone in the club and, in effect, opens the club's account with the broker.

Since the whole thing is strictly a voluntary arrangement, there's no restriction on the methods by which any club can make its investments; but the more successful clubs follow a procedure of careful study; regular monthly investments (plus plowing back all dividends received); elimination of trying to outguess the market; and reliance on the "dollar-cost-averaging" method of investment—of which there will be more later.

What happens at a typical club meeting is this: the roll is called; the minutes of the last meeting are read; the accounting member's report is presented; the monthly dues are collected; pending business is transacted; future study-committee assignments are made; time and place of the next meeting are decided;

the meeting is turned over to the study committee; the committee's recommendations (from suggested minimum of two companies and a maximum of five in any industry) are heard and discussed; the club votes on the recommended stocks (absent members voting by proxy), and, finally, the accounting member is instructed to purchase as many shares of the selected stock as the club's funds will permit. The books and papers are then put away and the gathering is free to turn into a dignified brawl.

The clubs are all free agents and if one of them wants to plow all of its money into penny uranium stocks every month there is certainly nothing to stop it—in which case it is suggested that you not call it an investment club but simply a sort of organized roulette game that doesn't involve buying a wheel. For the other clubs, however, one brokerage firm that has been very active in the guidance of budding investment clubs makes these general suggestions:

1. For the first 12 to 20 months study a new industry every month and buy a different stock from each every month.

2. After this period review what you have done and get better acquainted with the equities you own.

3. Be on the alert for opportunities to add to the stocks you already own.

4. Bring variety into your meetings by inviting an occasional expert on a certain industry or company to speak informally.

5. Visit the management of one of your companies and ask all the questions that weren't answered in the firm's annual report.

6. Try to schedule an occasional movie (nowadays most of the larger cities have a clearing office or booking station for the surprisingly large number of industrial films available on a loan basis to such groups), or have a general investment talk by your broker.

7. Don't, for Heaven's sake, take the whole thing too seriously. Remember, it's supposed to be a social as well as an educational sort of thing so don't get grim about it or it will stop being fun. One of the biggest causes of mortality among investment clubs, as a matter of fact, is the tendency of the group to break into cliques: the "heigh-ho" members and the "this-is-a-serious-business-so-knock-off-the-funny-stuff" faction. It can get pretty sticky if you don't watch it.

13

The Solitary Dabbler: The MIP

I HAVE in mind the formation of this company that would devote itself to the welfare of those people who are always saying: "Well, I'd really like to save reguarly, but just never seem to get around to it. Or, as the French say, *'à combien doit-on affranchir ceci!'* What's for supper?"

For these people who, at least, *say* they want to save regularly, I propose the formation of a small company to be known as "Throttle, Inc." On the payment of a modest annual retainer, subscribers will be entitled to the services of an efficient goon squad which will visit his home once a month, carry him off, screaming, in a curtained limousine to his bank where, with a revolver in his ribs, he will be forced to write and cash a check for $50. My squad will then take this money and invest it in a nice growth stock in the subscriber's name. Thus, the whole anguish of trying to force himself to save will be taken out of the subscriber's weak hands. Of course, there are a few legal angles still to be worked out.

As a less painful alternative to this, one can always turn to the highly successful and popular Monthly Investment Plan which was cooked up just about five years ago by the New York Stock Exchange. For one thing, it spares you from trying to explain to the neighbors just why two dark men keep dragging you out of your house on the first of every month, and nips in the bud any rumors that you're the "front man" for a dog-stealing ring.

Essentially, as you may know, the MIP is simply an informal, nonbinding agreement between you and any recognized broker (who is, naturally, a member of the New York Stock Exchange) that you will send him a check for a certain amount of money—as little as $40 a quarter, in fact—periodically, which he will use to buy stock of your choice and hold for you in your name. In the event you decide on more than one stock, your monthly, or quarterly, checks will be alternated between them. No one, incidentally, comes around and clubs you if you miss a payment. You may hurt the broker's feelings, but that is all part of the brokerage game.

Aside from the social aspect, the MIP differs from the investment club in that the former is an individual long-range investment plan, while the club movement is more of an educational program with long-range investment as a sort of incidental side-attribute. The MIP, for one thing, assumes that you know enough about investments to know that "common stock" isn't a farmer's description of a run-of-the-mine cow.

Because the Monthly Investment Plan is so simple in its operation, the program has been even more successful than the NYSE dared hope—in spite of a rather messy recession that got under way just about the time the program was getting a good toe hold. Five years after it started, according to the Exchange, the plan had already stimulated the purchase of 2,850,000 shares of stock, representing a total investment of about $112,600,000. This adds up to about 163,000 individual plans, of which more than half are still going strong. They're still being formed at the rate of about 290 a day.

In actual practice, you simply sign an agreement with your broker announcing your intention, we'll say, of sending him

The Solitary Dabbler: The MIP

$50 a month which he is to invest in Old Bumbershoot Distillers, Inc. These purchases are credited to your account as they are made, but the actual certificates won't be forwarded—without charge—until you have accumulated 50 shares of the stock and request delivery. If you're the distrustful type and want the certificates sent to you more often, it can be arranged with a handling charge of $1.

The main objection one might make to this plan is that the purchase of one stock, month in and month out, is a poor way to get diversification. This, of course, is true except that it isn't necessary to confine yourself to one lone selection in setting up an MIP program.

Diversification—as long as you're going to keep harping on it—can be achieved in several different ways: You might, for instance, decide to invest $100 a month, putting $50 of it into a food company and $50 into an electric utility. Or, you might decide to switch around quarterly by putting the January, February and March investment into a tobacco company; the April, May and June investment into a chemical company; and the October, November and December investments into a heavy machinery company.

As in the case of the Investment Clubs, an MIP program's biggest advantage for the little investor lies not only in the discipline of making regular investments but in the practical application of an old-time investment principle known as "dollar-cost-averaging." In the final analysis, dollar-cost-averaging is probably about as close to a "perfect" investment plan as you can get, and—happily—it's the whole backbone of the MIP.

The theory of dollar-cost-averaging is simply this: periodically (monthly, quarterly, or what-have-you), you invest a set amount of dollars in X, Y or Z stock—or in all three. You've set the amount of money low enough so that you won't have to abandon your plan periodically because of being caught in a financial bind. Most importantly, you carry out the plan with a complete disregard for what the market is doing or what your individual stocks are doing. You're all guts, you understand?

When stocks are high—so goes the dollar-cost-averaging theory—your money buys proportionately fewer shares of stock, and when prices are low you are getting proportionately a greater number of shares. This, oddly enough, is the secret of the success of this deceptively simple scheme.

Let's say, for example (a horribly oversimplified example, I'm afraid), that every month you are buying $100 worth of shares in Mother Volga's Chocolate-Flavored Vodka Company over a turbulent six-month period during which the price per share drops from $100 to $35 and then back up to $50 at the end of the six-month period. Here's how your purchase record would look:

	Market Price	*Invested*	*No. of Shares*
January	$100	$100	1.00
February	$ 75	$100	1.33
March	$ 60	$100	1.66
April	$ 50	$100	2.00
May	$ 35	$100	2.85
June	$ 50	$100	2.00

So, at the end of six months under the dollar-cost-averaging plan you would have invested $600 in 10.84 shares of stock for an average price per share of $55.35.

Suppose, though, that you had merely decided to buy two shares of the same stock each month over the same six-month period. How would you have come out?

Well, in January you would have paid $200 for two shares; in February, $150; in March, $120; in April, $100; in May, $70, and, in June, $100. Thus, in six months you would have

The Solitary Dabbler: The MIP

accumulated 12 shares of stock and laid out $740—or an average of $61.66 a share as against only $55.25 a share under the dollar-cost-averaging plan.

The strength of this investment principle, of course, lies in the fact that it ignores peaks and valleys in the fluctuation of stock prices, which means that you're prevented from overloading on stock at times when it tends to be overpriced and you automatically accumulate more at times when it tends to be underpriced.

No impractical theory, a recent study of dollar-cost-averaging as it might have been applied in a long-range program of accumulating General Motors stock showed that $500 invested quarterly since 1936 would have meant an investment, as of 1958, of $36,500. But you would have had stock at that time worth $146,225—a gain of 300.6 per cent. The same plan carried out in the purchase of Tri-Continental Corporation stock between 1939 and 1958 would have given you holdings worth $230,400 on an investment of $36,500—a gain of 531.8 per cent.

There are pitfalls in dollar-cost-averaging, of course, and one of the worst is biting off more than you can chew. Thus, you may be forced to stop buying right at the time when the plan is just beginning to work to your advantage—so you end up with a loss.

Two other pitfalls in dollar-cost-averaging (and thus, in the MIP plan) are: (1) a purely psychological one—you have to keep on buying even though the market may be in a slump and all you hear is gloom-and-doom talk. This is the sort of staying power that takes more nerve than you can possibly imagine. (2) Picking a stock that doesn't have the growth factors it's supposed to have.

In the latter case, for instance, $500 invested quarterly since

1939 in Woolworth stock would have given you, in 1958, holdings valued at only $32,400 for the $36,500 invested, an 11.2 per cent loss. So, while it is "near perfect," dollar-cost-averaging isn't infallible, unfortunately.

Nevertheless, the popularity of the MIP plan quite properly continues to zoom, thanks to such features as: (1) the fact that no credit is involved; (2) the fact that payments may be as low as $40 a quarter—less than $4.45 a week; (3) the automatic reinvestment of dividends (a feature of nine out of 10 MIP plans); (4) the lack of fees other than the standard 6 per cent commission on plans involving purchases under $100; (5) the provision of custodial charges for MIP shares without extra charge; and (6) the absence of penalties for missing payments.

Outside of being born rich, nothing could be more simple!

14

The Sinking Ship: When to Sell

WHEN there's silver in those golden locks and you kick the baseball back to the boys in the vacant lot instead of throwing it, will your heart still go pitty-pat when someone mentions a certain name?

By "certain name," of course, we mean "Consolidated Inter-American Parakeet Seed" (ticker symbol: BRAACK), a hot little issue pawned off on you by an idiot brother-in-law who affects Baruch-style pince-nez and velveteen spats.

Being a gullible soul, you have taken this dog to your bosom and, over a period of several years, have managed to convince yourself that it's the jazziest little number since Amerada Petroleum hit the market at 50 cents a share. Worse yet, you insist on puffing it up to all your friends and have turned into such a bore that you've been dropped from your three favorite clubs and your United Fund committee chairmanship.

The love affair that frequently builds up between an investor and his stocks is one of the sweetest romances you'll find this side of a high school prom. It seems almost impossible for many people to own anything without getting emotional about the thing—even just plain silly—and stocks are certainly no exception.

Of course hanging onto a stock is about the only way that anyone except a hardened, lucky and very rich speculator can hope to make money out of the stock market. But to say that you should buy the stock and then protect it like a spawning salmon is carrying what starts out as a sensible piece of logic to a ridiculous extreme. Teeth are nice too, but there's nothing very admirable about hanging onto them after they start falling apart in every hot cross bun you eat.

Psychologists know all about this reluctance to sell stocks and at the drop of a hat will tell you what it really means. Largely, the reluctance to sell a dog stems from the fact that the sale is the final, flat admission to the world, your broker and everyone else that you've been wrong. And, unfortunately, in the case of widows (where this sort of thing is found so often) the reluctance to sell an inherited stock is frequently a refusal to part with a link to the past—which simply defeats the intention of the dead husband in buying the stock in the first place.

At the other end of the scale, of course, it's even sillier to brood about the thing all the time and wind up switching your holdings back and forth with every rumor, news story, "reliable tip" and tea-leaf reading to which you are exposed.

The arguments are impressive against switching in and out of the market in an attempt to do better than the averages are doing, and the most convincing one is that it requires about 30 years of study, a giant intellect and the mad luck of a 75-year-old tightrope walker to break even on such a policy. You will hear about people who "are doing it all the time and making a real killing," but just who these lucky devils are never seems quite clear.

Probably the greatest practical argument against trying to trade in and out of the market lies in the fact that success requires a sort of "educated anticipation" and will power that not

The Sinking Ship: When to Sell 105

one person in 100,000 possesses. Ideally, the theory is to buy at a stock's low point, hold it a few months, then sell at its high point. This assumes that you know where this low point is and then have the courage of your convictions to go against the experts, whose evaluation of the stock's poor standing is the chief reason for it's being low, and buy it in the face of all the well-qualified reasons floating around for not buying it. The same sort of expert timing is needed, of course, in selling it when you figure that the time has come.

Obviously, the chances of your being right while practically everyone else is wrong about the stock, aren't nonexistent, but they sure wouldn't make for very good odds in the average floating crap game. Even when, in theory at least, you're right in guessing that a stock is about to make an upswing, or is about to decline in price, the all-too-human tendency is to wait just a bit longer in the hope of getting a more favorable price. Thus, at the bottom, you hold off a bit when the price of the stock hits 15 in the happy notion that you can pick it up for 14 by waiting a day or two. Instead, it eases up to 15, 17 and then to 18 before you finally give up the hope that it will slip back down to 14. And so you buy it for 18—your greed having cost you three points in the process.

On the upside, naturally, the tendency to wait just a whit longer for a better price is even stronger. Wouldn't you feel like a fool if, having bought it at 18, you watched it go up to 25, sold when it dropped to 24, only to watch it bounce back up to 35? And so you wait for it to bounce. It doesn't. It slides on down to 22 before you sell out and take a profit—a profit that is hardly worth the fretting, the worrying and the big gamble to which you exposed yourself.

To confuse intelligent, justified selling with this sort of skittishness is pretty ridiculous although it is widespread among investors who consider themselves in the market "for the long haul." If not necessary, occasional weeding out of dogs in your holdings is, at least, highly desirable.

But once you've steeled yourself to the project, how in the world do you know which stocks to sell?

First, according to the experts, anyone who doesn't review his holdings at least once a year has no more business in the market than he does in professional skeet-shooting with 20/400 eyesight. This doesn't mean that you have to get rid of some stock every year (although there's a school of thought that clings to this philosophy), but it does mean that you should look them over carefully at least that often. What are you looking for? a drop in the dividends? a drop in earnings? a slip in the price-earnings ratio? tearstains on the certificates?

A drop in dividends, of course, is a demoralizing factor, but to sell on this basis alone is pretty silly. Why have the dividends been cut? Maybe it's just plain caution, a desire to hold back more reserves than are normally carried in order to weather suspected rough spots ahead. Maybe it's being done to retire some old debts that have been hanging over the company. Such a move can mean even more funds available for melon-splitting in the years ahead. So just how serious is a drop in earnings? Possibly, but not necessarily, more serious than a cut in the dividends. Maybe earnings have dropped because the company has incurred heavier than usual expenses in getting a new plant or process into profitable production or in channeling more money than usual into research or product development. As a rule, unless the company really has its head in a bucket, all of these things spell better times ahead once the nonrecurring expenses encountered in getting them launched are out of the way.

In the case of both dividends and earnings, of course, you have to take the general business picture into consideration. So

The Sinking Ship: When to Sell 107

your pet company has shown lousy earnings for the last couple of quarters and has cut its dividends 75 per cent? This is really significant if the rest of the economy has been on the upswing in that same period and if your company has no ready explanation as to why this situation should prevail. But if everyone else is in the same boat, why be such a grouch about your own firm?

Weakness in the price-earnings ratio, on the other hand, is a considerably more serious affair. This ratio, incidentally, is determined by dividing the prevailing market price of the stock by the earnings accrued in the last year. Thus, if Consolidated Inter-American Parakeet Seed is currently selling at $38 a share and earning $2 a year the stock is said to have a P/E ratio of 19.

For the market as a whole, a computation of the P/E ratio (as it applies to the averages) is a pretty good yardstick of the public's confidence, or lack of it, in over-all business conditions. Thus, in times of recession when investors are pretty shaky in their attitude toward stocks, you'll find—on the average—that the P/E ratio stands at about 10 or less. This implies that the average investor is willing to pay no more than $10 for every $1 in earnings. And, at the other extreme, you'll find in a real "boom" market—when everyone feels that the sky's the limit on stocks—that the average investor will happily pay as much as $35, $40 or $45 in order to get back $1 in earnings.

Generally speaking, most level-headed authorities in the field feel that anything higher than $20 or $25, in order to get back $1 in earnings, is being optimistic to the point of complete ridiculousness.

In the same way that the P/E ratio is a good measure of the public's confidence in the market as a whole, so is it a pretty good yardstick of how most investors feel about individual companies—although in this respect we should note that a severe drop in the P/E ratio has considerably more significance than a big increase.

Suppose, for instance, that when you bought your shares in Conolidated Inter-American Parakeet Seed it was selling at 19 times earnings ($38 a share to get back $2 in earnings). Since then, we'll say, it has dropped to the point where it is selling at only 12 times earnings—in other words, the earnings have gone up to $4 but in spite of this the price of the stock has dipped to $36 a share.

Although the stock should be a better buy now since it is probably paying a higher dividend, something is obviously wrong; the price of the stock certainly hasn't reflected "improvement." This, then, is the time to start digging around to find out exactly why the company has lost so much investor-confidence. Underneath the surface, in nine cases out of ten, the wise boys in the market who watch such things like hawks have found a bug.

Have sales fallen off drastically? Why? Have operating costs soared without any apparent reason? Have inventories risen to a dangerous level? Has the net working capital shrunk drastically without logical reason?

A "yes" answer to any of these questions could mean a deterioration of management and possibly serious trouble ahead. Don't sell purely on the basis of a "yes" answer here, but do take the problems to your broker and tell him of your suspicions. If he knows of a reasonable explanation for the change in the price-earnings ratio, he'll tell you.

Otherwise, he'll help you dismount from that poor, dead horse.

15

Hedging Your Bets

Apart from the fact that he is inclined to have the squints from reading stock market tapes in poor light, the broker is probably a pretty nice fellow—nervous, perhaps, but nice. If your daughter started bringing him home for dinner there is even the possibility that you might give your blessings to the venture.

Once you yourself are involved in the stock market, the broker can become an even nicer person to have around. Besides his usual business of buying and selling securities for you and of keeping you well informed on both market trends and on individual securities that should be called to your attention, he can be of invaluable assistance to you in carrying out other well-known market stratagems. And, in at least a couple of these, he becomes almost a partner in the whole transaction.

Probably the two best-known techniques used in the market in which the broker plays such a dominant role are in the fields of margin buying and in the carrying out of "stop-orders."

Margin Buying——"Margin" could be, of course, a strip of wasted space along the edge of a piece of paper.

There's another definition of the word, of course—the one we're primarily interested in—but for several years after 1929 it had such a shameful connotation that you didn't use it unless your wife was out of town. It was in the great debacle of 1929, '30 and '31 that the very mention of the word "margin" was sufficient to send strong men into a state of quivering terror. It was the playful, friendly pup of the 1920s that suddenly turned and bit its master's hand off just short of the elbow.

You may remember that for the first six months after the 1928 election of Herbert Hoover any grumbling that the economy wasn't as healthy as it looked on the surface was enough to get a man stoned in the street. Prosperity was a great one-way boulevard leading everyone, from the plug-hatted financier to the bootblack, right up the golden ladder to an enchanted land where even the butlers would have butlers.

It was a typical "final" phase of a dynamic bull market—the era when the public catches the money scent on the breeze and starts forcing the price of all securities up to ridiculous heights. It led to asinine situations where a stock that never had earned more than a dollar a share would be selling on the market for $45 or $50 a share.

But, in the final analysis, it was the prevailing practices in marginal buying that brought the stupidity to a head.

Essentially, of course, buying stock "on margin" means nothing in the world but buying "on credit," and in its pure form it is about as nasty as paying $10,000 down on a $20,000 house and settling the rest in monthly installments. Pretty wicked, eh?

Never a plaything of the small investor who is only half sure of what he's doing, margin buying comes into being when an investor has satisfied a broker of his financial responsibility. The broker then will take a down payment on stock purchases and make up the difference out of his own pocket. How big the down payment must be has always been the sore point of margin buying, but the decision today rests with the Federal Reserve Board and the New York Stock Exchange and varying policies

Hedging Your Bets   111

established by individual brokers. The first two legs of this tripod—the FRB and the current role of the NYSE—were, significantly, not in existence back in the '20s. Chiefly because they exist today, buying on margin has ceased to be the dirty word it was 25 years ago.

What happened back in those days that kicked the props out from under credit buying and touched off the trek to the window ledge that so many brokers and investors took?

In the main, it was a matter of philosophy that got the dizzy spiral under way in the late '20s. The idea that the stock market could crash was unthinkable. For this reason, margin requirements—if we can flatter them by implying that there were requirements at all—were a bit on the flabby side. Margin requirements of only 20 per cent of the selling price were common and, if you were a good customer or had married the broker's daughter, the requirement frequently slipped down to 10 per cent. The "pyramiding" of purely paper profits became as socially acceptable as bathing.

Roughly, it worked this way: Your broker trusted you because of your big, baby-blue eyes; when you spotted a likely looking stock selling at $50 a share, he bought the stock for you with only a 10 per cent margin payment from you in actual cash. Thus, if you bought 200 shares you were paying only $1,000 in cash and the broker was advancing a loan of $9,000 to you to cover the transaction.

It was a period of zooming stock prices so we'll assume that your $50 stock went up to $80 in short order. If you sold out at this point you would realize a $16,000 gross. Repaying the broker his $9,000 left you $7,000 profit which you promptly reinvested with the same easy 10 per cent down payment. We'll say, this time, that you bought 1,000 shares of Amalgamated Andiron at $70 a share and, again put up only 10 per cent of the price ($7,000) while your broker obligingly put up the other 90 per cent ($63,000). Let's say that your good luck held out and that the stock went up from $70 a share to $90—a common occurrence at the time. Again you sold out, repaid the broker his $63,000 and still had $27,000 for further reinvestment. And so, at that point, you found yourself in a position to buy $270,000 worth of stock on that original $1,000 investment.

Don't think for a moment that there weren't plenty of speculators around in mid-1929 who hadn't parlayed just as little money into similar million-dollar paper empires. At the height of the foolishness there were more than 300,000,000 shares of stock being carried on margin, and margin accounts represented 40 per cent of the brokerage business being done in terms of volume, and much more than 40 per cent in terms of dollars.

When Black October 29, 1929 broke and more than 16,000,000 shares hit the market for whatever they would bring, the brokers got hot on the telephone and began demanding more cash from their margin accounts to cover the 90 per cent limb on which they were so precariously sitting. The customer didn't have the money—the profits were all on pretty scraps of paper —and so to cover the gap the speculators had to sell the only thing they had, the paper stock certificates. This, in turn, merely knocked prices down even further, which meant that more selling was necessary, which, in turn . . . and so.

Even the blue chips under this kind of pressure began faltering, and General Electric dropped from 396½ on September 3 to 210 on October 29. American Telephone and Telegraph dropped 100 points, and DuPont plunged from 217½ to 80.

In the light of this background it's hardly any wonder that a lot of brokers and investors were still gagging at the very mention of margin 15 years later. It has taken almost 30 years of

Hedging Your Bets

heavy-handed control over the thing to give back margin buying its respectability.

The biggest lever over margin buying is exercised by the Federal Reserve Board which has been given the okay by Congress to set minimum margin requirements. It jockeys these around in direct proportion to how worried the board is about the degree of speculative fever in the air. Since the big flub of 1929, the lowest that the down payment requirement has been was 40 per cent, a figure that prevailed from 1937 to 1945. The highest that it ever has been was 100 per cent, a figure in force from January 1946 to February 1947. And we're due for a return to this figure at any time—no margin buying at all, in other words. It was in 1958 that the FRB hiked the requirements from 70 per cent to 90 per cent as stock market activity again picked up sharply from the 1957 recessions.

As chummy as you are with him, your broker doesn't extend even 90 per cent margin to you just for the pleasure of watching your eyes light up with happiness. He extends margin to you because he charges you interest on the loan (comparable to existing rates anywhere), and this income is an important part of any brokerage business. Thus, while he certainly has no desire to get suckered the way he was in 1929, the broker understandably frets about extremely high requirements; at 90 per cent margin there is so little purpose in not buying the stock outright that this source of his income shrivels to virtually nothing.

Under your margin agreement with the broker, he has a fair amount of security in the loan today because he retains the stock and can use it at the bank to float loans of his own in order to carry your account and others like it. Since the dividends are in your name and the broker has nothing to gain if the stock rises sharply, it's only right on the other hand that he shouldn't be obligated to absorb any loss that the stock may rack up. Thus, under the New York Stock Exchange's rules, the broker must call on the customer for more margin—"cash," as we know it down here on the pool-room level—whenever the amount that the customer would have left if he sold his stock and paid off the broker's loan comes to less than 25 per cent of the current value of the stock. With 90 per cent margin requirements, of course, this business of having to call for more margin money is pretty uncommon because a 20-dollar-a-share stock would have to plummet to about $2.75 a share before your proceeds, after paying off the broker's loan, would leave you with less than one-fourth of the stock's selling price.

For the moment, then, buying on margin at today's high requirements has very limited application to most of us but is one of those techniques of stock buying that may profitably be used in the future when the current fear of excessive speculation cools off.

The Stop-Order——Assuming that you're on very good terms with your broker it is always possible, I suppose, for him to consent to a deal under which you would rent cot space from him in his board room. You could send a boy out for sandwiches occasionally, shave and dress in the washroom and, except for the cracker crumbs you've strewn over the cot, life might well go on in the brokerage just the same as usual. But for the bulk of us obsession with the stock market still doesn't override the necessity to go about our regular business, leaving the financial world, and our own interests in it, to fend for itself, unwatched.

With an uncommon number of investors, there is the same hesitancy about going out of town for a couple of weeks, leaving investments at the mercy of the market, as there is in going away and leaving the children with a baby-sitter who has shown up with Sen-Sen on her breath.

We'll assume, for instance, that about a year ago you bought

Hedging Your Bets 115

100 shares of United States Carmel Apples, Inc., at $30 a share. It turned out to be the smartest thing you had done since eloping with the town millionaire's only daughter 20 years before. USCA, a real sleeper, immediately romped up to $45. All the same, at the moment you are in a quandary.

On one hand—always—is your wife, who insists that you knock off work for a couple of weeks and take in the ceremonial grape-stomping at Naples. On the other hand is the disturbing knowledge that the price of USCA's stock has been wavering just slightly and that there is the distinct possibility that the floor could fall in while you are cavorting around Europe with your mouth full of corks.

The first solution to come to mind is that of selling. If you've been worrying over nothing, this simply means that you've got yourself out of a highly profitable stock with only a part of the profit that you might have realized if you'd kept your big fat hands off it.

Fortunately such a drastic step isn't necessary, thanks to a bit of market mechanics first approved by the Exchange more than a half-century ago. This is the "stop-order"—formerly known as the "stop-loss order," a name that has been abandoned not only because it wasn't quite accurate but because it sounded like a line from a high school dramatic production.

In effect, a stop-order is an instruction left with a broker to buy, or sell, a stock as soon as its market price hits a predetermined level.

In the case mentioned, for instance, you could leave instructions with your broker to sell your 100 shares of United States Carmel Apple "at 40 stop, good until cancelled." You could then take off on vacation with an unfurrowed brow, knowing that even if your stock slips below its present level of 45 you still have a handsome profit protected by the stop-order.

What happens after you're off, willy-nilly, is this: your broker, who has other things to do, sends the stop-order to the trading floor. Here it is turned over to a sort of broker's broker, a specialist in this business who is, oddly enough, known as a "specialist." His services, incidentally, cost you nothing. If the stop-order is executed for you his fee comes out of the standard charge made by your own broker.

The specialist enters your stop-order in his book and keeps a keen eye on USCA's fluctuating price. We'll say, for illustration, that you have no sooner disembarked at Naples and caught your first case of dysentery than USCA's price starts slipping and sinks from 45 to 44½ to 42 to 41⅜ and finally to 40. At this point the specialist swings into action and handles your stop-order just as your broker would handle a routine market order —he tries to get you the best price he can.

Things move fast on the floor. There may be other sell orders ahead of yours, so there is always a strong possibility that he won't be able to get it sold at exactly the $40 level you wanted; he may have to take 39⅝, 39½ or even a flat 39. It will be better, at any rate, than coming home to find your whole profit wiped out.

Stop-orders can also be used to protect a profit in a short sale. Let's say that you have sold 100 shares of Consolidated Goodies short at $75 a share in the hope of buying it back at a cheaper price. By the time you are ready to go on vacation the price has, indeed, dropped to about $60 so that you already have a profit of $15 a share. To protect this, you leave an order to "buy 100 Consolidated Goodies at $65 stop."

In this case you were again wise because the stock rallies and sneaks back from 60 to 65, wiping out little bits of your profit all the way up. With your stop-order in, the specialist buys 100

Hedging Your Bets

shares at, say, 65¼, and by covering your short sale has salvaged a good chunk of your profit.

The same sort of procedure can be used in the case of odd-lot transactions (orders of fewer than 100 shares), except that the odd-lot differential has to be figured in. Since odd lots aren't handled on the trading floor, but are handled by special brokers who, in effect, are retailers of less-than-100-shares, their "markup" for this service is ⅛ point, or 12½ cents a share, for stocks selling under $40 and ¼ point, or 25 cents, for those selling higher.

In the case of an odd-lot stop-order to sell at 30, the procedure is the same as described earlier for a 100-share lot except that you automatically forfeit another ⅛ point in the process as the odd-lot broker's fee. Thus, in executing a stop-order at 30, the transaction is actually made at 29⅞—or as close to it as possible.

Stop-orders obviously can't exactly pin your loss down, but they can keep it within fairly defined limits. For peace of mind, who's going to quibble over one point?

16

The Haggle Market: Over-the-Counter Stocks

Man and boy, for 85 years, the White Fang Happy-Mouser Cat Food Company has operated profitably as a purely family enterprise. From cat food the company has branched out into dog food, fertilizers and related products, and net sales are now well over $1,000,000—required expansions having been financed directly out of good old Granddaddy Fledgely's mattress depository.

Let's say that today's management is faced with the sticky proposition of either increasing its production and aiming at a bigger slice of the market or, in the face of an awkward price squeeze, of pulling in the company's horns and trimming the sales force. To latch onto a bigger slice of the market is going to require at least one and possibly two more complete processing and canning lines—an expansion estimated at about $500,000. And, frankly, the current tax setup has seriously crippled the family's old ability to reach into the mattress and pull out big wads of money at will.

Instead, the family gets its heads together with the state securities commissioner and, after complying with all the rules and regulations, issues a block of 5,750 shares of stock selling at $100 a share. This, which the local underwriter peddles to people who are familiar with the White Fang Happy-Mouser Cat Food Company, is enough to raise the required $500,000 and allow enough to cover the broker's fees for selling it (normally about 15 per cent of sales). In spite of the fact that the family still controls the company through ownership of previously issued private stock, it takes the firm forever out of that elite circle known as the "privately owned manufacturing company." This group shrinks appreciably in size every year.

By Dun & Bradstreet's most recent estimate there are about 2,900,000 American firms that either buy or sell something, the vast majority of them being little retail stores and similar one- or two-man affairs. But tens of thousands of firms are owned at least in part by the investing public, ranging in size from firms with a few thousands of dollars in capitalization to giants worth billions. Only about 3,500 of these organizations list their stocks on any of the country's stock exchanges. The rest make up that formless mass of private enterprises whose stock is traded "over the counter."

The greatest peculiarity of this whole market, and it is, indeed, as much of a market as the New York Stock Exchange, is that no one knows much about it. It is known that about 3,500 dealers operating in about 551 American cities and towns are actively engaged in the buying and selling of securities, the names of nine-tenths of which probably aren't even known outside the dealer's own city. No one knows for sure, but the daily volume of money changing hands in over-the-counter stocks is generally assumed to be many times over the total money volume handled on all of the stock exchanges put together.

Unlike the major exchanges, this over-the-counter market depends wholly on "negotiated" transactions rather than on the auction-type bidding with which we are more familiar.

Let's say that you've heard about the White Fang Happy-

The Haggle Market: Over-the-Counter Stocks 121

Mouser stock issue and that you'd like to buy about 25 shares of it—your cat speaks highly of the product. In the first place, you won't find it listed in your newspaper under the New York Stock Exchange or American Stock Exchange tables. There's only about one chance in 10, as a matter of fact, that you'll find it listed under "Local Investment," "Local Securities," "Over-the-Counter," or any of the other classifications used for this sort of thing. This may seem like a conspiracy of silence, but the fact of the matter is that there isn't a periodical in the country able to cope with the publication of "going" prices for over-the-counter securities; no one even knows for sure just how many such securities there are. About the closest approach to a listing of prevailing prices is a bulletin published daily by the National Quotation Bureau which contains the latest price information on from 5,000 to 10,000 of the more active over-the-counter securities.

Thus, when you call your broker and tell him of your hope to buy 25 shares of White Fang Happy-Mouser at 98—$98 a share—the procedure he follows is far different from that undertaken by a broker dealing in a listed stock. In the latter case he simply takes your order, forwards it to the Exchange where it is consummated and, in return, charges you a commission on the transaction.

The over-the-counter dealer, for one thing, may actually have some White Fank stock on hand (or, as he would put it, he has a "position" in it)—in the same way that a grocery keeps a few cans of anchovy paste around. Since we'll say for illustration that he doesn't have any White Fang at the moment, he'll take your order and promise to call you back.

The average over-the-counter dealer, incidentally, might just as well go to work in his underwear since practically no one ever walks into his office. A good 98 per cent of his work is done on the telephone or by the private wire network connecting many dealers in the same sort of work. Thus, as soon as he has your order, he begins making calls to fellow dealers, brokers, banks or heavily invested individuals and finally locates a dealer who mentions a client expressing an interest in selling some of his White Fang to meet a tax payment.

Your broker then contacts this individual and finds that he is quite willing to sell 25 shares of his White Fang stock at $95 a share. The broker then makes the purchase at this price and turns around and sells it to you at 98—for a profit to himself of $75, a shade over 3 per cent of the sale price.

Here we have one of the major differences between the operations of a conventional broker and those of the over-the-counter dealer. The former's remuneration is through a commission schedule that is tightly controlled by the New York Stock Exchange. The over-the-counter dealer, on the other hand, charges, in effect, a mark-up on the price of the stock. This profit margin incidentally, is controlled only by the insistence of the National Association of Security Dealers—one of the most effective voluntarily self-policing groups in the country—that the mark-up be a "fair" one.

You can't really pin it down much closer than this, the NASD feels, because unlike conventional exchanges where orders are simply forwarded to be executed at clearly listed prices, the over-the-counter dealer's profit should, rightly, be in relation to such factors as: the prevailing market for the stock being sought; the cost of the security; the amount of the transaction; and the availability of the security. He should, obviously, make a bigger profit on a transaction that involves making 50 telephone calls and necessitates three days of work than he will receive on selling a stock that he can pull out of his bottom desk drawer.

One study made of some 14,747 over-the-counter transac-

The Haggle Market: Over-the-Counter Stocks 123

tions showed that 79.5 per cent had been handled at less than 5 per cent mark-up and that 43 per cent had cost the customer less than 3 per cent. In general, where mark-ups exceeded 5 per cent, a large number of the transactions were in low-priced securities. After all, there's more work in gift-wrapping a dozen lima beans than in tying up a stack of four-dollar steaks.

Conscious that an over-the-counter dealer's position in the financial community is only as good as his ethical record, the NASD is rough on members who wander from the straight and narrow. Fines, suspensions and expulsions are potent weapons which the NASD doesn't hesitate to use when necessary. The group's board of governors has heard many times before all the slick excuses for overcharging.

It's true that many big investors scowl down their noses at the over-the-counter market. It's often slower and much clumsier to dispose of such stocks in an emergency because a market for them often doesn't even exist until a dealer gets on the telephone, makes some calls and creates the demand. And, of course, companies whose stocks circulate over-the-counter aren't subject to the very rigid examination and surveillance imposed on them by the major exchanges.

Nevertheless there are thousands of good, sound buys available over-the-counter that are just as desirable—in some cases, more so—than those listed on the major exchanges. And, for the really shrewd investor, there are hidden fortunes lying in the over-the-counter market: small companies just beginning to grow that may someday be considered the hottest "growth situation" of the twentieth century. Maybe.

At any rate, we don't buy securities, whether sold through the New York Stock Exchange or over-the-counter, that we haven't investigated thoroughly beforehand.

Do we?

17

How to Be a Sorehead: Selling Short

"CONFIDENTIALLY," you whisper to your dinner companion as your mutual friend, Fleekman, passes out of earshot, "Fleekman's sort of a jerk!"

"Oh, I don't know," comes the indignant answer. "Fleekman's got a lot on the ball. I wouldn't sell him short, if I were you! Can *you* build boats in bottles?"

If you'll re-read this, substituting "Amalgamated Ice Tong Company" for "Fleekman," you not only have a classic stock market situation but you are even employing a standard piece of stock market lingo—"selling short." In effect you are taking the historic roles of a "bear" and a "bull" in the market in your differing attitude toward a third party—in this case, Amalgamated Ice Tong.

As a bear you are roundly convinced that AIT has shot its wad—that its fortunes are due to slide, that its dividends will fall off and that the current market price of 25 is slated to tumble. You wouldn't buy it at that price if it meant gaining a juicy tax loss. Your friend, on the contrary, views Amalgamated Ice Tong as a good bet and feels that this price very likely will rise to 30 or even 35 in time. Eventually, you'll stop speaking to each other.

As a bull, your friend can express his faith in AIT by buying its stock and waiting for the price to rise. But what alternative do you, as a bear, have in expressing your opinion?

You can express your disapproval of AIT just as roundly by selling it short—the one avenue open to the pessimist in voicing his low opinion of a stock. The stock market, as in the case of any kind of market, can exist only as long as there is a constant buying and selling demand, and—in about three-fourths of all buy-sell transactions—a difference of opinion is the very reason why such trading is possible. For every case of an investor selling because he needs the money, there are some three other sales made for no other reason than that someone has become disgruntled and has decided to dump his stock in favor of another. And the simple fact that he is able to sell implies that there is someone, somewhere, who wants to own it as badly as he wants to get rid of it.

Without the short-selling technique you, as a bear, would have no way to express your belief that a stock is overpriced except by buying some and then turning right around and angrily selling it as a matter of principle. Except for the fact that it's a little asinine—like drumming your heels angrily on the floor—it's possible to do it, I suppose, even if you do get a reputation as a secret drinker.

Selling short, however, is a much more practical way of accomplishing this—and making a profit to boot. It is simply a process through which you go ahead and sell AIT, even though you don't actually own any, in the hope of buying back later at a lower price.

At first blush, of course, this business of selling stock that you don't own would seem to have all the ethical qualities of entering a game of chance with a pair of dice capable of rolling up-

How to Be a Sorehead: Selling Short   127

hill under their own power. Actually, the principle behind selling short is a gimmick far more common in day-to-day life than is generally supposed.

Let's say, for instance, that you're a tailor and a good customer comes in and orders a suit for fall delivery. You quote him a price of $125 and take a $25 deposit. In effect you have sold the suit "short" because you are gambling—oh, in a very, proper way—that you can make and deliver the suit at the $125 price. What if the price of wool suddenly skyrockets and you find that it's really costing you $130 to make the suit? Well, you take the loss like a big boy.

So, since you're so inflexibly convinced that Amalgamated Ice Tong's price of $25 a share isn't going to hold up, you call your broker and tell him to "sell short 100 AIT at the market." To show that you're a good fellow, you put up 90 per cent—or whatever the margin requirements are at the time—of the $2,500.

Your broker now finds a buyer at $25 and you, friend, have just sold 100 shares of nonexistent stock (stock that the parent company doesn't even know anything about, as a matter of fact) to a buyer who has bought them in good faith and expects you to deliver. Unfortunately, if AIT pops up a day or two later and declares a dividend you have no alternative but to pay this out of your own pocket to your buyer—a detail obligingly handled by your broker.

A week or two later, and good old AIT's price falls apart like a wet cracker just as you had predicted. It sinks, we'll say, to $20 a share and you smugly call your broker and tell him, "Cover my short position." The broker, in turn, goes on the open market, buys the stock at $20 and delivers it to the man who loaned it to you. Having bought at $20 and sold at $25 you pocket the 500-dollar difference, less commissions, for a fair profit. The procedure is simply the reverse of the conventional way of carrying out a buy-sell transaction.

On the other hand, if Amalgamated Ice Tong double-crosses you and begins to rise steadily from 25 to 27 to 29 to 30 to 33 to 35, you have considerable reason for dark mutterings. You can hang on indefinitely in the hopes that it will eventually slide back down under the $25-a-share level at which you sold it, and under which you must buy it for delivery in order to make a profit. As the price rises, of course, more margin is constantly required because you are not permitted—technically—to run "in the red."

Sooner or later, Buster, you're going to have to buy it, and the thing boils down to a matter of will power. Let's say that AIT gets up to 35 before your nerves fly apart at the seams. You call your broker and—good grief!—tell him to get you off the hook, but fast! He buys the stock at $35, delivers it to the man who bought it from you earlier at $25 and bills you accordingly.

All of this is a perfectly legitimate, and exciting, little aspect of dabbling in stock, but it hardly seems necessary to belabor the element of risk in it. In 1954 and again in 1958, when stocks started shooting up out of sight, the streets were knee deep with the tears of harassed "shorts." Some stubborn speculators have been known to "maintain a short position" in a stock for years, paying out dividends steadily and watching their losses soar up out of sight.

The professionals, as you might imagine, keep an eye on short sales like a sparrow stalking a grub. The New York Stock Exchange along in the middle of each month reports a detailed breakdown of just how many shares of each stock are in a "short" position as the end of the past month, and it affords everyone interested in this sort of thing with an excellent cross-

How to Be a Sorehead: Selling Short   129

section of that elusive quality known as "investor sentiment." Obviously, if the number of shares of United Things, Inc., sold short between April 15 and May 15 increases from 25,000 to 187,000 it indicates pretty strongly that a lot of investors got disillusioned with the stock. Just why they did may, or may not, be a pertinent question. The fact that so many investors sold United Things short might only mean that they felt that the price of the stock was due for a "technical correction"—a temporary drop—that would give them a chance for a quick profit. Or, of course, it could mean that they felt that the company had gone sour for some reason or other.

The importance of watching the number of shares in a "short" position lies in the realization that every share sold short means that, at some time in the future, one share has to be bought on the open market when the investor sets about to "cover" his short position. This has a dual significance. If the market price of the stock starts declining, then the number of shares sold short acts as a cushion under its drop. If it drops five points, for instance, a large number of investors who have earlier sold it short are stimulated into taking their profit—that is, they have to buy it. The purchase naturally serves to jack up the price of the stock a little and slows down the decline in the stock's price.

In a bull market, on the other hand, a large number of short sales outstanding in a stock serves in most cases to quicken the pace of the stock's climb. If, contrary to the belief of the investors who have sold United Things short at 35, the stock goes on up to 40, it naturally shakes a lot of them into buying it back before their fears of suffering a really stiff loss materialize. When they buy they naturally accelerate the stock's rise even more, which in turn scares more investors into buying, which in turn hikes the price, and which . . . and so on into the night.

Short selling is an interesting approach to the market and a lot of people have successfully used it in the past to make a pot of money. But these successful short sellers, it should be pointed out, have at least one very important thing in common: they have a nervous system chiseled out of living rock.

Unless you are the type who can continue chatting while picking a black widow spider off your arm, or feel a kinship to the passenger who insists on finishing the magazine page he is reading before the flaming airplane hits the bay, by all means keep out of short selling.

18

Signs, Symbols and Tiny Type

In a big, wide, wonderful world where people study caterpillars to determine the severity of the approaching winter and watch Gemini's ascendancy as a clue to their love life, it would be odd indeed if investors weren't bitten by the same bug.

The slight streak of larceny that exists in all of us nags away with the persistent suspicion that there must be—has to be—some foolproof way of determining where and when the stock market is going to jump next. And, as might be expected, some very ingenious self-styled experts are practically always on hand to give us—pardon, sell us—the magic formula.

Unfortunately, too, it is precisely at times like these in the market that such advisory services, as they prefer to call themselves, pop forth faster than baby guppies. Their advertisements in the financial newspapers and magazines make pretty racy reading: "Amalgamated Blight Due to Soar to 55 Area!" "Five Stocks for Fabulous Gains!" "Send for 12 Oil Issues Overdue for Dynamic Upswing!"

On the other hand, there are some statistical, well-established theories of long-range forecasting—such as the improved Dow Theory, the Parker method, the Lowry computations and a few others—that have proved themselves extremely useful when properly applied. The chief difference between these rational forecasters and the gypsies that promise quick, fabulous profits, is that the responsible forecasters concern themselves with spotting major shifts of the market's trend and not with short-range forecasting of specific stocks.

Let it be said here and now: there is no reliable way of predicting day-to-day, week-to-week or even month-to-month shifts in the direction of the market, and certainly there is no way of predicting when this or that stock will go up or down, or to what extent. There are so many factors going into why the market will bobble one way one day and the opposite the following day that it is foolish to pretend that anything better than a fifty-fifty record of accuracy in calling such shots is possible.

The quickie, crystal-ball-gazer's reputation of hitting the market's swings on the nose is self-created, as you may have suspected, by the simple device of calling attention to the times in the past when, by a fluke, he happened to be right for a few days and by conveniently forgetting the many, many times when he was dead wrong. You can have a real ball for yourself, incidentally, by going back to the library files of some of the financial newspapers and periodicals and looking up the issues appearing at the height of the 1957-58 Recession. Here you will find the crystal-gazers in the advertisements somberly offering, for rather handsome prices, selected lists of stocks that one should weed out before the market continues its slide to abysmal lows.

Needless to say, most of these pundits were caught out on a limb with a cross-cut saw a few weeks later when the market's upswing started in earnest and pushed to new highs the stocks that they had recommended selling. Oddly enough, their current advertisements make no mention of the fact that they successfully frightened who knows how many gullible readers into selling stocks at a terrific loss and then didn't change their tune

Signs, Symbols and Tiny Type 133

and start advising buying again until prices were 'way back up out of the bargain basement.

Of the several methods or theories for long-range prediction of market trends, probably the best known is the Dow Theory. In spite of the fact that a lot of people pawed over it with their grubby hands for several years and so grossly misused it that it lost a lot of its reputation for validity, it is still one of the more reliable methods of spotting over-all shifts in the market's trend.

Essentially, the so-called Dow Theory is simply a series of rather broad explanations about how and why the market shifts around. It had its start in the writings of Charles H. Dow, editor of the *Wall Street Journal* at the turn of the century. These ideas were expanded after his death by William P. Hamilton and Robert Rhea and their combined writings has come to be viewed, loosely, as the Dow Theory.

To explain in a very fragmentary way, Dow's idea was that the market moved like the ocean tide and was made up of three trends—the day-to-day movements which he likened to the lapping of small waves on the beach, larger intermediate swells that throw themselves forward on the sands and, finally, the strong dominating tides, of which both the small waves and the swells are a part. It was Dow's idea that the only element that really mattered in all this was the movement of the tide itself. By being able to recognize the signs that the tide was about to shift, the investor actually had all the knowledge he needed to come out of the market with a profit.

He felt that by keeping a keen eye on various aspects of the market the investor should be able to spot the beginnings of a bull market very early, buy good values and then sit tight on them, disregarding day-to-day and intermediate fluctuations. Four to eight years later—the average duration of most bull markets—the bearish shift in the tide should be apparent, Dow thought, and the investor would then take the opportunity to get out of the market with his profits and sit on the sidelines to await the turn of the tide.

Because Dow tied part of his studies in with a careful charting of the famous Dow-Jones averages—which he also founded—and was somewhat less than explicit in outlining the technical studies that should be made of the market's gyrations, the quacks moved in on the Dow Theory and started to apply it, willy-nilly, to an out-and-out study of the Dow-Jones averages alone. It was a hopeless oversimplification of what Dow meant and, as a result, countless self-styled Dow theorists began to interpret the Dow Theory without knowing its true meaning and ended up giving the whole concept such a black eye that it hasn't really recovered since.

Probably the best-known modern interpreter of the Dow Theory is E. George Schaefer, whose weekly publication *The Dow Theory Trader* has, in the last ten years, restored a lot of the respect to the sixty-year-old philosophy. While he bases his ideas on the writings of Dow, Hamilton and Rhea, Schaefer has applied his own technical studies to the subject and was the only major analyst to predict and to stay bullish throughout the current ten-year-old bull market. The best example of his bullish interpretations came in late 1957 and early 1958. Having for months dismissed the Recession as a mere consolidation of the long-term, major bull market and not, as virtually all other analysts had said, the beginning of a bear market, he predicted a vigorous resumption of the bull market before the market did exactly that.

Admittedly, the adherents of the modern Dow Theory and most of the other "formula" plans have to be patient souls who are willing to stick with a preconceived plan of action for 4, 8, 10 or maybe 15 years before making any really decisive changes in their stock holdings. This sort of patience isn't a widely held commodity, and so the pickings are ripe for the fly-by-nighters who move in with grandiose schemes for spotting market fluctuations on a day-to-day basis and offer glamorous ways of making big profits that require little—or, better yet, no—knowledge of why the market acts the way it does.

Take, for instance, the "Gridiron Method of Forecasting Stock Prices," which is described in Garfield A. Drew's *New Methods for Profit in the Stock Market*. Under this theory, which Drew recommends like a hole in the head, one needs only to keep up to date on Harvard-Yale, Army-Navy and California-Stanford football games.

If, in any year, the loser of the Harvard-Yale game fails to score, this is regarded as a "buy" signal for the next year—unless there is no difference between the points scored by California in the Stanford game and those scored by Army in the Navy game. You simply sell the year after California beats Stanford.

While the snickering dies down it might be added that if you had followed this system from 1920 to 1940 you would have netted about 600 points profit—and only two small losses—in terms of the Dow Jones industrial average. You would have known about the 1929 crash and sold out, then bought back in 1932 to ride the market up just prior to the sharp collapse of 1937.

It sounds terrific, but it pains me to report that when California beat Stanford in 1941 all of the gentlemen following this system sold their holdings in 1942 just in time to miss the big bull market swing that got underway then. In fact, they didn't buy back in until 1946 when prices were much higher.

Another briefly popular "analyst" went quickly out of business when it was revealed that he was basing his predictions on a highly complex interpretation of the action and dialogue appearing in a newspaper comic strip. And still another "theorist" bases his recommendations on a study of dog license statistics—reasoning that when people are optimistic and inclined to buy stocks (thus forcing prices up) they precede it by going out and buying dogs for the kiddies.

For sheer persuasiveness in this space age, it's pretty hard to beat the sunspot forecasters with their graphs and charts. They hinge their argument on the apparently correct assumption that everything in nature moves in cycles and hits periodic, foreseeable peaks—weather changes, for example, run in 11½-year cycles, the elephant population hits a peak every 62 years and our population of field mice is highest every fourth year.

From this jumping-off point the sunspot theorists come to the conclusion that sunspots, which occur every 11.2 years have a decisive influence on the stock market. And who, pray, is to argue?

Other cycle theorists simply chart the peak activity of various aspects of the economy—steel production or freight carloadings for instance—and draw their stock market conclusions from these complex computations. Unfortunately, even the cycle theorists themselves will admit that the market may be influenced by more than one series of cycles. There is, for instance, a 41-month cycle, a 9-year cycle, an 18½-year cycle and 54-year cycle—to name only a few of the more prominent cycles—and that any "buy" or "sell" indicators can be anywhere from six to nine months early or late. And this, mind you, is under the best of circumstances.

One of the more fascinating cycle theories ties the activity of the stock market to the world's increasing volcanic eruption and earthquake activity. Vesuvius, for instance, erupted just

Signs, Symbols and Tiny Type

before the severe depressions of 1873, 1907 and 1929. This earthquake and volcanic activity, incidentally, is supposed to be building up to a peak in about 1962—in case you'd like to start making a few plans.

Silly? Perhaps, but we must remember that they laughed at Dr. Frankenstein.

While a great deal of discretion has to be exercised in hooking one's star onto this theorist's pet beliefs or to that chartist's involved philosophy, there is probably more danger for the average investor in the simple process of picking up the telephone. Theorists, chartists and other professional forecasters, after all, are only trying to sell you their services, ranging all the way from a dollar or two for a trial subscription to several hundred dollars a year for the complete service. The "boiler room" operation, on the other hand, is trying to peddle a commodity that is far flimsier and normally costs a great deal more money.

A "boiler room," incidentally, is usually nothing more than a large room lined with men hunched over small desks. Each desk is equipped with the boiler room operator's stock in trade—a telephone—and frequently you will find that the desks are separated by sound-absorbent partitions or, lacking that, a cloth hoodlike arrangement which the caller can toss over his head to muffle the clatter coming from the rest of the room.

The boiler room operator's chief goal in life is to sell you stock over the telephone—99 times out of a 100 a stock that you never heard of, but almost invariably a stock in one of the "glamour" industries: uranium, oil, electronics, gold or what-have-you. The job isn't really so tough as it sounds, human greed being what it is, because the boiler room operator, quite aware that a verbal sales talk is flimsy evidence in court when the defendant chooses to deny that he said any such thing, is pretty free to throw around just about any sort of extravagant promise that pops into his fertile little head.

You will find, for instance, that he "got your name from a mutual friend" (who, incidentally, he'll be so coy about mentioning that he never will name him) because he knows that you'll be interested in a wonderful opportunity opening up for a limited number of small investors. The "opportunity," as it develops, will turn out to be 100 shares of the Happy Gusher Exploration Company stock which is still "on the market" at only $5 a share. He confides mysteriously this is possibly because the newspapers haven't yet "got wind of what's going on out there," and so the public, as a whole, hasn't heard about last week's strike—500 barrels a day if there's a drop!

By this time the boiler room operator figures, pretty safely, that he's got you panting and he swiftly closes the deal. You send him your $500, receive in return an impressively printed certificate, and if you ever hear of the stock again you can at least count yourself that much luckier than most victims.

Regardless of whether the salesman hits you with a glowing proposition over the telephone, in your office, on the street corner, or suddenly turns up one night at your home, you can guard pretty well against being scalped if you follow the advice currently being plugged by the Securities and Exchange Commission and the Better Business Bureau, to wit:

(1) Think before buying.
(2) Deal only with a securities firm you know.
(3) Be skeptical of securities offered over the telephone from any firm or salesman you don't know.
(4) Guard against high pressure.
(5) Beware of promises of quick, spectacular price rises.

Signs, Symbols and Tiny Type

(6) Be sure you understand the risk of loss as well as the prospect of gain.

(7) Get the facts—not tips or rumors.

(8) If offered securities over the telephone, tell the caller to send you the firm's prospectus giving all information about the stock, its backers, and the like.

(9) If you don't understand the prospectus when it comes, take it to someone who does.

(10) Give as much thought to the stock purchase as you would to a piece of land or an automobile costing the same amount of money.

Lastly, don't fall for the old line that "you haven't got much to lose," because the stock being offered sells for only 10 cents a share. One thousand shares of this is still $100, anyway you slice it—whether it's represented by 100 shares, 50, 25, 10, 2 or 1. If you lose it, remember, it's still a hundred hard-earned bucks.

19

Palmistry and Head Bumps: The Seers

Poor old Aunt Borinda—there she lies, stiff and cold. Done to death by a shuffleboard puck! And you, as the sole heir, become the lucky possessor of three cats, a curtain stretcher, a tear-stained mah-jong set and, incidentally, 5,000 shares of Consolidated Carpet Tacks—currently paying a dividend of about $2.35 a share annually.

As a new stockholder, two courses are open to you. You can, first, put the stock certificates safely away, forget about them, and go back to your job in the duck decoy factory. The only trouble with this system is, while your back is turned, Consolidated Carpet Tacks runs into rocky times and you suddenly find, instead of banking the usual $11,750 a year that has been turning up in the mail, that a subtle change has taken place. You end up the year banking a check for $75 that the company sends wrapped in a piece of brown butcher's paper.

The alternative is to learn something about stocks, the market and market news so you can keep a halfway intelligent eye on how things are going over at the tack factory. Appearances to the contrary, it isn't nearly so complex, or even boring, as you may have been led to believe.

The place to begin your education in following the market—

as everyone who hangs around brokerage offices sniping cigarette butts calls it—is on the financial pages of your daily newspaper. A big evolution in journalism has occurred in this section of America's newspapers. Only in relatively recent years have editors become aware of the fact that there is far more interest in this sort of news than they ever thought possible. As recently as 10 years ago financial news was still brushed off as little more than an obligation that the newspaper was duty-bound to "cover." Normally a financial editor was assigned this section of the paper on the basis of his inability to hold down a decent job anywhere else on the staff. And so, naturally, he put his financial pages together with all the care and discrimination of a mink hitting a brood house.

Fortunately, the staggering increase of interest in the stock market has dragged along with it a great hunger for all other related financial and business news and—sensitive to the charge that their coverage of this sort of thing had all the spark of a road surveyor's report—the management of today's newspapers have, in most cases, thoroughly reshuffled the whole setup.

Most daily newspapers, for instance, carry at least some sort of table of activity on the New York Stock Exchange, as well as less extensive listings on the American or Midwest stock exchanges and additional listings of local, over-the-counter stocks. How completely the newspaper goes into this sort of thing is directly traceable to both the editor's concern with complete coverage and the amount of space he can afford to devote to the subject. Many, unfortunately, are pinched badly in the matter of newsprint today and are limited to a pretty sketchy listing of the individual stocks. A typical table of listings in a newsprint-short paper usually includes only: (1) the price at which the stock closed on the preceding afternoon (or on that afternoon in the case of evening newspapers going to press an hour or two after

Palmistry and Head Bumps: The Seers 143

the market's closing), and (2) the change in price this figure represents from the closing price of the preceding day. Depending on the individual newspaper's taste, fractions are expressed either in decimals representing ⅛ of a dollar—12½ cents—or in fractional multiples of ⅛: ⅛, ¼, ⅜, ½, ⅝, ¾ or ⅞. A newspaper economizing on space might carry this listing:

NatCashR   64-.7

National Cash Register's stock thus closed on this particular day at an even $64 a share, a decrease of 87½ cents a share from the closing price of the previous day.

Fortunately, most of today's metropolitan papers—and, of course, such purely financial newspapers as the *Wall Street Journal*—carry far more expanded market quotations. Here for example is how the *Wall Street Journal* handled National Cash Register's listing on another day of trading:

1959 High	Low	Stocks	Div.	Sales in 100s	Open	High	Low	Close	Net Chg.
80	62¼	NCashR	1.20	29	63⅜	64⅜	63⅜	64⅜	+1

The reader is told that National Cash Register had a fairly uneventful day of trading during which volume of stock trading hands was moderate—2,900 shares. And, after opening at $63.375 a share, stock moved slowly but steadily up $1 a share to end the day at its high point of $64.375 a share. From the table we can also see that National Cash Register on this particular day was trading only slightly higher than its low for the year ($62.25) and was still a long way from regaining ground held earlier this year—$80 a share. We also learn that, so far, the company has paid out $1.20 a share in dividends—based on current annual rate.

This sort of coverage—all of it comprising less than two and a half inches of type—gives a tremendously broad picture of a stock's past and present performance in an amazingly small amount of space. But, in sympathy with the many newspapers in the country that can't devote this much space to listings, it has to be fairly admitted that the average small stockholder can make do very well with the abbreviated form mentioned earlier.

Since the stock market leans so heavily on abbreviations, symbols, decimals and what-have-you, it's only natural to find this carried to an even greater extreme in the broker's office itself, where the ticker tape constantly spews forth a stream like this: SKF 2s48⅛ AME4s52⅞ SX70 ¼ . . .

For brevity each stock listed on the exchange has its own ticker symbol and there's simply no point in trying to make much sense out of many of them. Some abbreviations do suggest the stock they represent: GM (General Motors), GE (General Electric), PA (Pennsylvania Railroad), KO (Coca Cola), SKF (Smith, Kline and French) and ZB (Crown Zellerbach).

Just as many symbols bear no relationship at all to the stock they represent: X (U.S. Steel), L (Sinclair Oil), DT (American Radiator), FD (Central Foundry) and LT (National Lead).

The numbers following the symbol refer to the hundreds of shares involved in each transaction and to the price per share. Odd lots—sales and purchases amounting to fewer than 100 shares—aren't shown, so a ticker showing GM49½ simply means 100 shares of General Motors were traded at $49.50. The reading GM6s48⅞ would mean 600 shares of General Motors had been traded at $48.875 a share. At 1,000 shares, however, the number of shares is spelled out all the way: GM5.000s48½ (there are periods only on the ticker) means 5,000 shares were traded at $48.50.

The jumble of fast-moving symbols, abbreviations and numbers that flash out is pretty confusing at first, even though the actual tape is in most brokerages magnified and transmitted to a large screen above the quotation board so that the whole room can watch it without having everyone trampled insensible in the process of trying to read the tape as it spews out of the ticker. As the symbols begin to make sense, the experience of sitting there watching millions of dollars change hands every few minutes can exert a hypnotic effect that makes it difficult to pull away. Some of the characters seen in the country's brokerages today, in fact, give the appearance of not having been out for a decent meal—or a bath—in the last 15 years.

One of the peculiarities of the stock market, indeed, is the speed at which the whole dizzy process can get into your system. Ownership of five shares of U.S. Bottle Stoppers, Inc., has been known to make avid readers of the *Wall Street Journal* out of people who haven't read anything more constructive than the fine print on the back of baggage claim checks for the last 20 years.

Simply following the ups and downs of one or two stocks eventually gets to be pretty tame stuff and at about this point you run headlong into the confusing matter known around the better poolrooms as "The Averages." No one really admits that discussing the stock market's health in terms of averages is entirely satisfactory—the "average" stock, for one thing, is pretty hard to find. It also brings up the old argument that a six-foot man can easily drown in a stream having an "average" depth of only eight inches.

Unfortunately, though, averages are about the only workable way to keep a finger on the pulse of the market and so we're stuck with them. Thus, if you ask a broker today how the market went yesterday, you'll get an answer that may sound like this: "Up one-oh-eight!" or "Off point-thirty-two."

The broker is of course talking in terms of the Dow-Jones industrial stock average—the oldest and most universally accepted system of stock averages in use. To translate, the broker is saying that the market rose $1.08 (or lost 32 cents, in the other example) during the course of yesterday's trading.

While the Dow-Jones averages certainly have their critics, the wide acceptance they enjoy is traceable to the fact that they were the first to be computed hourly during the five-hour trading day, and were originated by the Dow-Jones Company, which prints the *Wall Street Journal*—the country's top financial newspaper.

Other accepted averages that have sprung up and have their own bands of followers include the Associated Press averages; the New York *Times* averages; the New York *Herald-Tribune* averages; and Standard and Poor's stock index, based on the hourly selling price of 500 stocks and computed electronically.

In actuality, the Dow-Jones average is really four averages—those of 30 leading industrial stocks, those of 20 leading railroads, those of 15 leading utilities and a composite average of all 65 stocks used. Of these, the 30 industrial are the most important and it is this average that the broker has reference to when he tells you that "the market was off 32 cents today."

When the whole thing began back in 1896, the Dow-Jones industrial index was made up only of 12 important issues. There is probably a moral for all us fragile humans in the fact that most of these "vital" stocks aren't even remembered today. What, for instance, ever happened to American Cotton Oil, Standard Rope and Twine and some of the other leaders of 1896?

Today—after lo! the many, many substitutions that have been made as one stock is assumed to have become "more representative" of the over-all industrial picture than another—the

30 stocks making up the Dow-Jones industrial average are: Allied Chemical, Aluminum Company of America, American Can, American Tobacco, Anaconda Company, AT & T, Bethlehem Steel, Chrysler Corporation, DuPont, Eastman Kodak, General Electric, General Foods, General Motors, Goodyear, International Harvester, International Nickel, International Paper, Johns-Manville, Owens-Illinois Glass, Procter & Gamble, Sears Roebuck and Company, Standard Oil of California, Standard Oil of New Jersey, Swift & Company, Texaco, Union Carbide, United Aircraft, U.S. Steel, Westinghouse and Woolworth.

To arrive at the Dow-Jones industrial average the selling prices are added together and then divided by 3.964. The same method of computation is used in arriving at the other Dow-Jones averages except that the total price of the 20 rails is divided by 5.601; the total price of the 15 utilities is divided by 8.53; and the composite average is determined by adding together the selling price of all 65 stocks used and dividing by 19.61.

Without getting too involved in mathematics, it should be pointed out that these divisors—3.964, 5.601, 8.53 and 19.61—are factors introduced by the economic experts to counterbalance the effect that stock splits, stock dividends and occasional substitutions of one stock for another in the averages would otherwise have. Without such a flexible formula, for instance, if Union Carbide split its stock two-for-one it would show up the following day selling—not at its usual 141 or 142—but at about 72 or 73. This would throw the whole Dow-Jones industrial average into a terrific, but purely artificial slump unless the mathematically formulated divisor was adjusted to account for the radical change in Union Carbide's selling price.

Stock splits, after all, do not basically change the total value of a company's outstanding stock. They are simply a device by which a company puts more of its stock into circulation as a means of stimulating trading in it—investors, being only human, prefer to have 500 shares of a stock worth $20 a share than 50 shares worth $200 a share. It is common practice in the market to cater to this taste by doubling or tripling the number of outstanding shares when the prices get "too high" for popular consumption, but at the same time adjusting the price per share to compensate. Thus a firm having 1,000,000 shares of stock currently selling at $150 a share on the market might authorize a two-for-one stock split which would give each shareholder two new shares for each one he now holds. In this way, for the 50 shares (worth $150 apiece) which you now hold, you would be issued 100 shares having a value on the market of about $75 apiece.

When this happens to one of the stocks making up the Dow-Jones averages, then, some mathematical adjustment obviously has to be made to account for the halving of the price; it is done by developing a new divisor.

The averages, of course, aren't going to do you any more good in making a profit on the market than a yardstick will in making your suit long. But—just as in following the progress of a football team—keeping an eye on the ground lost or won makes the whole game a lot more interesting.

20

Technical Studies: Reading the Pulse

For sheer puzzledrone, the specialized language in which the stock market has wrapped itself makes shoptalk between two nuclear physicists sound like recess at the kindergarten.

For the layman, one of the more irksome manifestations of this is found frequently in those financial news stories where the author blithely tosses off something like: "The stock market advanced on a broad front today as technical strength made itself felt." It has a nice lilting ring to it, but what in Heaven's name does it mean?

This business of tossing in little phrases such as "technical strengths," "technical weaknesses," and "technical market factors" is—as, heh! heh! we were guilty of, ourselves, a few pages back—a sort of lazy way of saying that many of the man-invented gauges by which investors try to predict the significance of the market's behavior tend to lean this way or that way. "Technical factors," then, are situations existing in the market itself by which investors try to judge not only the health of the market but also its probable direction.

A conscientious investor armed with his own pet "technical yardsticks," you try to measure the market with them in very much the same way that economists use the more tangible business indicators,—such as employment figures, car loadings, steel output and installment loan totals—to arrive at a picture of existing business conditions.

There are almost as many technical indicators as there are traders on the market and everyone has his own particular set of favorites. They range in validity all the way from excellent down to highly suspect, or even worthless. And, theoretically at least, it should be possible on some bright day for someone to stumble across the exact combination of technical factors that would give him the precise picture of what the market is going to do next. And then, of course, the whole thing would stop being any fun for anyone.

Whether you're analytical-minded enough to give a good whoop about looking up market data required in a technical study of price trends, is immaterial. You really should know what some of the more common technical indicators are and what they mean, just so you won't get a glazed look in your beady eyes when your broker starts dropping them into the conversation.

Here are the ones that pop up most often:

Investment Buying—Of primary interest to any analyst who hopes to predict the trend of the market is the activity of the big investment buyers, the so-called "smart money" operators who have an excellent record of buying at the right time and selling at the right time. About the only firsthand way to keep an eye on whether investors are beginning to buy into the market is by plopping yourself down in a broker's office and watching the size of the transactions as they flick across the ticker tape screen.

One way to get the same information is by watching the published figures showing the ratio between odd lot buying and odd lot selling—this, since an odd lot is less than 100 shares, is a

Technical Studies: Reading the Pulse 151

pretty good indicator of what the little investor, or the general public, is doing. And, with a little analysis you can deduce pretty well from the published activity of the small investors what the big ones are doing.

Suppose, for instance, odd lot selling is running a great deal heavier than odd lot buying. Normally, of course, such an out-of-balance situation should drive prices down because supply is clearly exceeding demand. What if it doesn't work out that way? What if, in spite of a preponderance of odd lot selling, stock prices are reflected in the Dow Jones industrial average continue to go up?

Well, it's pretty conclusive evidence, in a situation like this, that someone is quietly snapping up the surplus supply as soon as the odd lot sellers get rid of it and is keeping up the prices. And this "someone," obviously, couldn't be anyone but the big investor. Naturally, the thing works exactly the same way in reverse. If the volume of odd lot buying is much heavier than odd lot selling, but in spite of this prices keep dropping lower and lower, it is pretty apparent that large investors dealing in round lots are selling heavily enough to drive prices down by keeping supply ahead of the odd lotters' demand.

From a technical standpoint, then, the fact that investment buyers are slipping quietly back into the market—or just as quietly out of the market—is highly significant because these are the experts who must be presumed to know, or suspect, something that the rest of us don't.

The Broad Base———You'll hear and read a lot about how "the broad base of the market suggests an upswing of significant proportions." As you may have guessed, this "broad base" is a favorite technical factor of the analysts who put a lot of faith in charts that depict the market's day-to-day progress in terms of the averages. There is more reason for paying attention to the broad base theory than the mere fact that it makes an interesting pattern on a chart. The theory behind the broad base is that, like a human, the market can jump up higher only if it "rests" occasionally and then gets a running start.

Thus, the longer the Dow-Jones industrial average drifts along in a more or less horizontal line without significant ups or downs, the more firm and broad the market's base is said to be, and the more "poised" it is—technically—for an upsurge. Forgetting the chart business for a minute, the broad base theory is important because just as nature abhors a vacuum, so does the stock market—as represented by millions of investors and speculators—abhor inactivity. It is grossly unnatural for the market to drift horizontally for very long; the longer it resists going down, the better the chances for its going up.

Dividend Yield——Keeping an eye on the average dividend yield offered by common stocks selling on the market is a longstanding custom of extreme importance. It only stands to reason that as a bull market expands and as stock prices rise to high after high, the average dividend yield that can be realized, in ratio to price, is going to drop steadily. Profits, except in very rare cases, aren't going to rise as fast as stock prices in a bull market for fairly obvious reasons.

To reverse the logic, it's only natural to expect the ratio between the yield on the stock and its market price to go up when the price of the stock slips sharply. Earnings, on which dividends are based, are relatively stable whether the price of the company's stock has shot up to $85 a share or has plummeted to $40 a share. Thus, at the bottom in 1932, stock prices had dropped so low that even against the trimmed-down dividends being distributed the dividends still represented, on the average, a 10.3 per cent return on the investors' money.

As times improved this average dropped—to 7.9 per cent in

Technical Studies: Reading the Pulse

1942, to 6.9 per cent in 1950, 4.8 per cent in 1958 and to 2.93 per cent in mid-1959.

Normally—and quite logically—the investor's ardor toward stocks cools as the dividends drop; somewhere along the line it becomes possible to shift his money over into investments that offer a return that is almost as good as, or better than, he could get on stocks. When this realization hits a big segment of the investing public you are apt to see stocks go into a nose dive as investors pull their money out of the market and go into bigger-paying investments. The big question is: just where is this point of realization? Fortunately, we've got some historical precedence to fall back on here.

When the big bull market fell apart in 1929, the average dividend of the Dow-Jones industrials was down to 3.1 per cent; the bull market in 1937 terminated when the average yield was down to 3.7 per cent, and in 1946 it cracked when the average yield was down to 3.2 per cent. So, from a technical standpoint, the market is assumed to be on the shaky side by most investors when the average yield of the 30 Dow-Jones industrials dips under the 4 per cent-a-year-level.

All of which is hardly very comforting, is it, with the average yield on stocks at the lowest point in years? So, why hasn't the bottom fallen out?

Probably the best answer as to why investors haven't viewed the current low yield of stocks too seriously is that today's high prices on stocks are being paid in anticipation of much higher company earnings (and thus dividends) in the months ahead. Those who argue that stock prices are not yet alarmingly high insist that rapidly increasing dividends will soon swing this ratio between yields and prices into line. If, of course, earnings and dividends don't improve as much as expected, there could be trouble.

Another explanation of why investors show no great desire to shift from relatively low-paying stocks into bonds, lies, as you may have expected, in the fear of continuing—perhaps indefinite—inflation: a state of mind that leads a lot of investors to the conclusion that, difference in yields be damned, common stocks still have a much better chance than bonds do of keeping abreast of the cost-of-living.

Odd Lot Short Sales——A "short sale" occurs when an investor sells stock he doesn't own at today's prices and hopes to buy the stock at a lower price than he sold it. The whole thing is a sort of promissory note speculation—you sell 100 shares of Amalgated Curry Brushes at today's price of $50 on the speculation that the price is about to drop. Sure enough, it does, and in about three months when the price has dropped to $35 you "cover" your transaction by buying 100 shares at this lower price, delivering it to your buyer, and pocketing a $1,500 profit —less commissions, naturally.

An odd lot short sale simply means that this sort of transaction has taken place in a lot of less than 100 shares—a clear indication that a small investor has taken himself a flyer. Shrewd investors take a more than passing interest in these figures (which you'll find listed in most financial publications, such as the *Wall Street Journal* or *Barron's*) for a strange and, in many ways, cynical reason.

The small investor who buys for the long haul is one thing, but the small investor who is also a speculator—buying in and out of the market and selling short for a quick profit—is, if you'll pardon the expression, a horse of another color.

Historically, the small investor who speculates has always —as a group—proved almost 100 per cent wrong. At least that's the way that most big investors figure, and so they watch odd lot short sales in the belief that the market is about to take

Technical Studies: Reading the Pulse

off in a direction opposite to that expected by the vast majority of small speculators.

It's pretty hard to figure the logic of this, but most large investors realize that the little speculator is influenced almost entirely by what he reads and hears about business conditions. The little spectator forgets—or didn't know in the first place—that the current market has discounted today's business and is anticipating tomorrow's conditions. Thus, when the commentators tell him that everything has gone to pot, he sells short just in time to watch the market creep back up and cause him a sharp loss.

Cynical though it may be, the big boys watch the little speculator and when he sells short they buy. Toward the end of a bull market, the thing starts working in reverse. As soon as odd lot short sales drop off to a trickle, it's a pretty good sign that it's time to sell—so much optimism on the part of the little speculators is considered pretty suspicious.

For the short run—a few months—this theory is not infallible, but in the long run the small speculator who dabbles around in short selling has a record of being almost invariably wrong.

Resistance Level——In the final analysis, the use of phrases such as: "The market today successfully penetrated its resistance level of 650 in the Dow-Jones industrial average" (an arbitrary figure used as an example) is one of the most common technical indicators thrown out by financial writers. It's also one with a great deal of validity.

In essence, a "resistance level" indicates the point in the Dow-Jones industrial average (or in any of the other commonly accepted averages) where prices once before broke and went into a decline. In practice, it doesn't become a true resistance level until the decline in prices has stopped, recovery has set in, and—for the second time—the prices climb to about the same area, only to fall back once more. It's almost entirely a psychological sort of thing.

Being human, investors are inclined to be worriers. The big question in their minds is: "How high can prices go before the market cracks again?" Obviously, the best answer they have available to them is the clear, historic record of how the market went on its last upswing before breaking. As the market recovers from a decline and begins working its way back up, nervousness naturally increases as it approaches the level at which it last cracked.

Rather than take a chance on a loss (remember, they bought into the market when prices were lower), speculators tend to sell out as the average approaches its last high point and take a small profit on the deal. The selling drives prices down and, sure enough, they end up contributing to the very thing that they feared—the market indeed breaks once more at the "resistance level."

It's an odd thing, but even when the stock market is on historically high ground and, theoretically, offers no precedence for a resistance level, investors simply get around this by inventing a new resistance level out of whole cloth. As when the industrial average was bobbling around that awesome thing—"the 600 resistance level in the Dow Jones average." Never having been as high as 600 before, and certainly never having broken there before, this resistance level was simply plucked out of the air because the experts felt that it was a logical place for the market to run into some selling pressure. It marked, for one thing, a jump from the 500s to the 600s—an area never even approached before—and students of the market guessed that it would make investors nervous. Which it did.

The significance of all this resistance level business should be fairly obvious—once such a level has been penetrated (not

Technical Studies: Reading the Pulse 157

just on one day, but on two or three in a row), it's a pretty good indication that investors no longer consider it a logical ceiling on how high stock prices can go. A bit of reverse psychology then takes place and the market normally reacts like an intercontinental missile hitting its second phase.

Penetration of a stubborn resistance level is a highly bullish sign and the effect on the market is that of a powerful shot in the arm. Acceleration is apt to be pretty breathtaking for a while until threats of another resistance level arise.

In the light of the technical indicators that we've investigated here, it's fairly obvious that today's long bull market—while still booming—is growing old and has a fairly limited life span. No bull market can continue indefinitely and when we take into consideration that this one, for all intents and purposes, began nearly 11 years ago, and that the average life span of a bull market in market history is between six and eight years, it only stands to reason that this one should be showing signs of wear around the edges. Whether the dropoff, when it comes, will be as severe as it was in 1929, and will be followed by a major depression, or whether it will simply drift moderately lower, as it did in 1958 when it hesitated to catch its breath, no one can know.

There are interesting profits still to be made in today's bull market on a short-range basis. And, on the long-range outlook, following a major readjustment—in terms of 15 or 20 years, that is—the future is as bright as it has ever been. We are in one of those unusual periods in history when the thoughtful investor should be able to play both ends against the middle with a very high chance of success. He should be able to make some profitable "quickie" investments within the next year, pull in his horns in preparation for the decline that is inevitable, and then hop back into the market for the long haul at prices that, in another 10 to 20 years, he will look back on as ridiculously cheap.

The industrial potential of this country, after all, has hardly got off the ground yet and it is today's careful investor who will pluck the fattest grapes in the years ahead.

Brief Topical Index

What the market is and how it started, 11

Why invest? 19

The broker's function, 27

What do you want in a stock—growth, income, stability? 33

Bonds and classes of preferred stocks, 41

Stocks for both income and limited growth, 47

How to tell a growth stock, 53

The various ways of speculating, 59

Stocks of top-grade safety, 69

Mutual funds; "open-end" and "closed-end trusts," 75

Why and how stock is listed, 83

Investment clubs: who they're for and how they work, 89

Monthly investment plans; dollar-cost-averaging, 97

When to sell; the P/E ratio, 103

Margin buying and stop-orders, 109

Over-the-counter stocks; the NASD, 119

How to sell short and why, 125

Reading about stocks; the Dow Theory, 131

Market analysts and prophets; the listings; the averages, 141

Technical indicators in the market, 147